Learn to Speak™

Spanish DELUXE

REFERENCE BOOK

The Complete Language Learning System

Donna Deans Binkowski, Ph.D.
Eduardo A. Febles, M.A.
Daniela Melis, M.A.

Based on original content by:
Cynthia Duncan, Ph.D.
Charles J. Bruno, Ph.D.
Martin P. Rice, Ph.D.

382161–MAN/1103kg

How To Use Your Workbook

The *Learn To Speak* program will be your principal tool for gaining listening comprehension and conversation skills, but this text can serve as a handy reference tool for vocabulary and grammar questions, as an aid during your conversations with the onscreen characters, and as a workbook for reviewing and practicing grammar.

The text is organized into eight major sections which have been marked by tabs to facilitate access:

Basic Expressions contains all the expressions introduced in the *Basics Course* of the program. Use this section to review and practice common phrases. You may also want to refer to this section as you practice branching Conversations with onscreen characters.

Story and Action contains the dialogues from all the lessons in the *Comprehensive Courses*. Use this section to review the dialogues and to practice your reading skills. You may also want to refer to this section as you practice branching Conversations with onscreen characters.

Grammar contains a reference grammar. The content of the grammar largely coincides with the content and organization of the *Grammar Guide* in the program. Use this section to learn about specific grammar points, such as the Present Tense of Regular Verbs, or to review entire categories, such as Verbs or Nouns.

Exercises contains exercises for selected grammar points. The exercises are drawn from the program content, but have been modified to fit a textual format. Use this section to practice your grammar when you are unable to use the program, and to see where you need more practice.

Answer Key contains the answers to the exercises.

Appendices contains handy grammar charts and a grammar glossary.

Vocabulary contains the vocabulary from your *Learn To Speak* program. It is arranged alphabetically according to the foreign language.

Indices contains alphabetical indices of selected grammar points and the *Story and Action* dialogues.

Contents

Grammar Topics 51

NOUNS 51

PRONOUNS 53

ADJECTIVES & ADVERBS 58

VERBS **64**

Basic Phrases
GREETINGS AND FAREWELLS

Greetings

Hola.	*Hi./Hello.*
Buenos días.	*Good morning.*
Buenas tardes.	*Good afternoon.*

Asking and Answering the Question "How are you?"

¿Cómo está?	*How are you? (formal)*
¿Cómo estás?	*How are you? (informal)*
¿Qué tal?	*How's it going? (informal)*
Muy bien, gracias.	*Fine, thanks.*
Más o menos.	*OK.*
Bastante bien.	*Pretty good.*
Estoy bien.	*I'm all right.*
¿Y usted?	*And you? (formal)*
¿Y tú?	*And you? (informal)*

Farewells

Hasta luego.	*Bye.*
Adiós.	*Good bye.*
Nos vemos.	*See you later.*
Bueno, ya me tengo que ir.	*Well, I have to go now*
Buenas noches.	*Good night.*

GETTING INFORMATION

Excusing Yourself

Disculpe. . . . .*Excuse me.*

Lo siento. . . . .*I'm sorry.*

¿Perdone? . . . .*Pardon me?*

Asking for Help

¿Dónde está el correo? . . . .*Where is the post office?*

Está allá. . . . .*It's over there.*

¿Qué quiere decir "limpiaparabrisas"? . . . .*What does "windshield wiper" mean?*

Quiere decir "windshield wiper." . . . .*It means "windshield wiper."*

¿Qué es esto? . . . .*What is this?*

Es una máquina de boletos. . . . .*This is a ticket dispenser.*

¿Cómo se dice "I love you" en español? . . .*How do you say "I love you" in Spanish?*

Te quiero. . . . .*"I love you."*

Usted habla muy bien el español. . . . .*Your Spanish is very good.*

¿Podría hablar más despacio, por favor? . . .*Could you speak more slowly, please?*

No entiendo. . . . .*I don't understand.*

¿Habla usted inglés? . . . .*Do you speak English?*

"Please," "Thank you," and Other Important Expressions

Un poco. . . . .*A little.*

¡Por supuesto! . . . .*Sure.*

Sí. . . . .*Yes.*

No. . . . .*No.*

No sé. . . . .*I don't know.*

Por favor. . . . .*Please.*

Gracias. . . . .*Thank you.*

De nada. . . . .*You're welcome.*

No hay problema. . . . .*No problem.*

De acuerdo. . . . .*OK; all right.*

Bueno... . . . .*Well...*

INTRODUCTIONS

Introducing and Being Introduced

Ésta es la Señora Gutiérrez.	*This is Ms. Gutiérrez.*
Me gustaría presentarte	*I'd like you (informal) to meet*
a algunos de mis amigos.	*some of my friends.*
Mucho gusto.	*Nice to meet you.*
El gusto es mío.	*My pleasure.*
¿Conoce a María?	*Do you (formal) know Mary?*
¿Conoces a María?	*Do you (informal) know Mary?*
Encantado/a.	*How do you do.*
Soy Miguel.	*I'm Michael.*
¿Cómo se llama usted?	*What's your name (formal)?*
Me llamo María.	*My name is Mary.*
¿Cómo te llamas?	*What's your name (informal)?*
Podemos tutearnos, ¿no?	*We don't have to be so formal, do we?*
Ha sido un placer.	*It was nice meeting you.*

GETTING ACQUAINTED

Talking about Your Country of Origin

¿De dónde eres?	*Where are you from?*
Soy de los Estados Unidos.	*I'm from the United States.*
Soy de Francia.	*I'm from France.*
Soy de México.	*I'm from Mexico.*
¿Eres americano/a?	*Are you American?*
Sí.	*Yes, I am.*
No, soy canadiense.	*No, I'm Canadian.*

Telling Someone How Long You're Staying

¿Cuánto tiempo te piensas quedar aquí? . . .	*How long are you staying?*
Dos semanas.	*Two weeks.*
Sólo por unos días.	*Just a few days.*
Un mes.	*One month.*

LEARN TO SPEAK SPANISH

Talking about How You Like the Country

¿Te gusta aquí?	*How do you (informal) like it here?*
¡Me encanta!	*I love it.*
¡Es estupendo!	*It's great.*
Pues, no tanto.	*Well, not so much.*

Talking about Work

¿En qué trabajas?	*What do you do?*
Soy ingeniero/a.	*I'm an engineer.*
Trabajo con computadoras.	*I work with computers.*
Cuido a mis tres hijos.	*I take care of my three kids.*
Soy modelo.	*I'm a model.*
¡Eres muy bonita!	*You're very beautiful.*
¡Eres muy guapo!	*You're very handsome.*
¿Te gusta tu trabajo?	*Do you like your job?*
Me encanta.	*I love it.*
¡Qué va! Es aburridísimo.	*Not really...it's boring.*
Más o menos.	*It's all right.*

Talking about School

¿Eres estudiante?	*Are you a student?*
Sí, estudio administración de empresas.	*I'm a Business major.*
¿Qué estudias?	*What are you studying?*
Estoy en la facultad de derecho	*I'm in law school.*
Biología.	*Biology.*

Talking about Leisure Activities

Para divertirte, ¿qué haces?	*What do you do for fun?*
Me gusta dar excursiones a pie.	*I like to go hiking.*
Me encanta viajar.	*I love to travel.*
Escucho música.	*I listen to music.*
¿Qué tipo de música te gusta escuchar?	*What kind of music do you like?*

Me gusta todo tipo de música menos . . . . . *I like all music except opera.*
la opéra.

Me encanta el jazz. . . . .*I'm into jazz.*

Y a ti, ¿qué te gusta? . . . .*How about you?*

¿Te gustan los deportes? . . . .*Do you like sports?*

Sí, me gustan. . . . .*Yes, I do.*

No, no me gustan. . . . .*No, I don't.*

Me gusta jugar al tenis. . . . .*I like to play tennis.*

MAKING FRIENDS

Expressing Interest

¿De veras? . . . .*Really?*

¡Qué bien! . . . .*That sounds great.*

¡Qué lástima! . . . .*Too bad.*

A mí también. . . . .*Me too.*

Offering and Asking for Something to Drink

¿Tienes sed? . . . .*Are you thirsty?*

¿Qué deseas tomar? . . . .*What would you like to drink?*

¿Te gustaría tomar algo? . . . .*Would you like something to drink?*

No, pero tengo hambre. . . . .*No, but I'm hungry.*

Una cerveza, por favor. . . . .*I'd like a beer, please.*

Un café, por favor. . . . .*A cup of coffee, please.*

Yo no quiero nada, gracias. . . . .*Nothing for me.*

Finding Out Who Someone Is

¿Quién es ése? . . . .*Who is that?*

Es el jefe de la compañía. . . . .*That's the president of the company.*

LEARN TO SPEAK SPANISH

Finding Out about Marital Status

¿Estás casado/a? . . . .*Are you married?*

¿Por qué preguntas? . . . .*Why do you ask?*

Por curiosidad. . . . .*I'm just curious.*

No, no estoy casado/a. . . . .*No, I'm not. (married)*

No, soy soltero/a. . . . .*No, I'm single.*

Sí, felizmente casado/a. . . . .*Yes, and very happily.*

Talking about Family

¿Tienes hijos? . . . .*Do you have kids?*

¿Tienes hermanos? . . . .*Do you have any brothers or sisters?*

Sí, tengo una hija. . . . .*Yes, a daughter.*

No, pero me gustaría tener algún día. . . . . .*No, but I'd like to someday.*

Tengo una hermana menor. . . . .*I have a younger sister.*

Asking about Age

¿Cuántos años tienes? . . . .*How old are you?*

Veintidós. . . . .*Twenty-two.*

Tengo treinta y un años. . . . .*I'm thirty-one years old.*

Cumpliré diecisiete el mes próximo. . . . . . .*I'll be seventeen next month.*

Adivina. . . . .*Guess.*

Asking Someone for a Date

¿Te gustaría salir conmigo uno de estos días? . . . .*Would you like to go out sometime?*

¿Te gustaría jugar al tenis conmigo uno de estos días? . . . .*Would you like to play tennis with me sometime?*

¿Qué tal mañana? . . . .*How about tomorrow?*

Vamos a comer algo. . . . .*Let's go get something to eat.*

Story and Action Dialogues

TRAVEL
Exchanging Money at the Bank

Story

Karen	Necesito cambiar dólares por pesos.	*I need to change dollars for pesos.*
Mario	¿Dónde está la oficina de cambio?	*Where is the exchange office?*
Empleada	La oficina de cambio está a la vuelta.	*The exchange office is around the corner.*
Karen	Necesito cambiar unos dólares.	*I need to change some dollars.*
Cajero	¿Cuántos quiere cambiar?	*How many do you want to change?*
Cajero	El cambio está a tres pesos por dólar.	*The exchange rate is three pesos to the dollar.*
Karen	Treinta dólares.	*Thirty dollars.*
Cajero	¿Cómo los quiere?	*How do you want them?*
Karen	En billetes grandes, por favor.	*In large bills, please.*

Action

Thomas	Perdón, señora.	*Excuse me, ma'am.*
Empleada	¿Dígame?	*May I help you?*
Thomas	¿Dónde puedo cambiar unos dólares?	*Where can I change some money?*
Empleada	La oficina de cambio está a la vuelta.	*The exchange office is right around the corner.*
Thomas	Gracias.	*Thanks.*
Thomas	Señor, necesito cambiar unos dólares.	*Sir, I need to change some dollars.*
Cajero	¿Cuántos?	*How many?*
Thomas	Treinta dólares.	*Thirty dollars.*
Cajero	El cambio está a tres pesos por dólar. Entonces, son noventa pesos. ¿Cómo los quiere?	*The exchange rate is three pesos to the dollar. So, that makes ninety pesos. How do you want them?*
Thomas	En billetes grandes, por favor.	*In large bills, please.*
Cajero	Aquí tiene.	*Here you are.*
Thomas	Muchas gracias.	*Thank you very much.*

7

Taking a Taxi

Story

Mario	Para ir al hotel, necesitamos tomar un taxi.	*To go to the hotel, we need to take a taxi.*
Mario	Buenos días. ¿Está libre?	*Is this taxi free?*
Taxista	Sí. ¿Adónde quiere ir?	*Yes. Where do you want to go?*
Mario	¿Por cuánto nos lleva al Hotel Internacional?	*How much do you want to take us to the Hotel Internacional?*
Taxista	¿Cuántos pasajeros?	*How many passengers?*
Mario	Cuatro.	*Four.*
Taxista	Treinta pesos.	*Thirty pesos.*
Mario	No, es demasiado. Le doy veinte.	*No, that's too much. I'll give you twenty.*
Taxista	No, no puedo por menos de veinticinco.	*I can't do it for less than twenty five.*
Mario	De acuerdo.	*O.K.*
Taxista	Ponga las maletas aquí atrás.	*Put your luggage here in the back.*
Mario	Gracias.	*Thanks.*
Taxista	De nada.	*You're welcome.*

Action

Thomas	Taxi, ¿está libre?	*Is this taxi free?*
Taxista	Sí. ¿A dónde quiere ir?	*Yes. Where do you want to go?*
Thomas	¿Por cuánto me lleva al Hotel Internacional?	*How much do you want to take me to the Hotel Internacional?*
Taxista	¿Cuántos pasajeros?	*How many passengers?*
Thomas	Yo solo.	*Just me.*
Taxista	Treinta pesos.	*Thirty pesos.*
Thomas	No, es demasiado. Le doy veinte.	*No, that's too much. I'll give you twenty.*
Taxista	No, no puedo por menos de veinticinco.	*I can't do it for less than twenty five.*
Thomas	De acuerdo.	*O.K.*
Taxista	Ponga las maletas aquí atrás.	*Put your luggage here in the back.*
Thomas	Gracias.	*Thanks.*

Checking into a Hotel
Story

Karen	Buenos días. Tengo reservada una habitación a nombre de Karen Santiago.	*Good morning. I have a room reserved here in the name of Karen Santiago.*
Recepcionista	Lo siento, pero no encuentro nada aquí.	*I'm sorry, but I don't find any record of it*
Karen	Necesito una habitación para cuatro personas, con baño privado. ¿Cuánto cuesta?	*I need a room for four people with a private bath. How much will that be?*
Recepcionista	¿Por cuántos días?	*For how many days?*
Karen	No sé. Unos quince días.	*I don't know. About fifteen days.*
Recepcionista	Entonces le podemos hacer un precio especial. Cincuenta pesos diarios.	*Then we can offer you a special price. Fifty pesos a day.*
Recepcionista	Este precio incluye el desayuno.	*This price includes breakfast.*
Karen	¿No tienen habiatciones más baratas?	*Don't you have less expensive rooms?*
Recepcionista	Hay habiatciones más pequeñas pero sin baño privado.	*There are smaller rooms, but they don't have private baths.*
Karen	Déjelo, preficro pagar un poco más y tener baño privado.	*Leave it, I prefer to pay a little more and have a private bathroom.*

Action

Thomas	Buenos días. Tengo reservada una habitación a nombre de Thomas Smith.	*Good morning. I have a room reserved here in the name of Thomas Smith.*
Recepcionista	Lo siento, pero no encuentro nada aquí.	*I'm sorry, but I don't find any record of it.*
Thomas	Necesito una habitación para una persona, con baño privado. ¿Cuánto cuesta?	*I need a room for one person with a private bath. How much will that be?*
Recepcionista	¿Por cuántos días?	*For how many days?*
Thomas	No sé. Unos quince días.	*I don't know. About fifteen days.*

continued...

Checking into a Hotel
Action: continued

Recepcionista	Entonces le podemos hacer un precio especial. Cincuenta pesos diarios. Este precio incluye el desayuno.	*Then we can offer you a special price. Fifty pesos a day. This price includes breakfast.*
Thomas	¿No tienen habitaciones más baratas?	*Don't you have less expensive rooms?*
Recepcionista	Hay habitaciones más pequeñas pero sin baño privado.	*There are smaller rooms, but they don't have private baths.*
Thomas	Déjelo, prefiero pagar un poco más y tener un baño privado.	*Leave it, I prefer to pay a little more and have a private bathroom.*

Room Service
Story

Botones	¿Dónde pongo las maletas?	*Where should I put the suitcases?*
Karen	Póngalas al lado de la cama, por favor.	*Put them next to the bed, please.*
Botones	¿Está todo bien? ¿Necesita algo más?	*Is everything alright? Do you need anything else?*
Karen	Sí, espere un momento. No se marche. Necesito jabón, toallas y agua mineral.	*Yes, wait a minute. I need soap, towels, and mineral water.*
Botones	Muy bien. Ahora se lo traigo todo.	*Fine. I'll bring them to you right away.*
Mario	Tengo hambre. ¿Puede decirme dónde puedo comer cerca de aquí?	*I'm hungry. Can you tell me where I can eat near here?*
Botones	¿Prefiere comida norteamericana o mexicana?	*Do you prefer American food or Mexican food?*
Mario	Nos gustaría comer algo mexicano.	*We'd like to eat something Mexican.*
Botones	Hay un restaurante bastante bueno al otro lado de la calle. Se llama "El Tampiqueño."	*There's a fairly good restaurant right across the street. It's called "El Tampiqueño."*
Mario	Muchas gracias. Aquí tiene.	*Thanks a lot. Here you are.*

Room Service
Action

Botones	¿Dónde pongo las maletas, señor?	*Where should I put the suitcases, sir?*
Thomas	Póngalas al lado de la cama, por favor.	*Put them next to the bed, please.*
Botones	¿Está todo bien? ¿Necesita algo más?	*Is everything alright? Do you need anything else?*
Thomas	Sí, espere un momento. Necesito jabón, toallas y agua mineral.	*Yes, wait a minute. I need soap, towels, and mineral water.*
Botones	Muy bien. Ahora se lo traigo todo.	*Fine. I'll bring them to you right away.*
Thomas	Un momento. No se marche. ¿Puede decirme dónde puedo comer cerca de aquí?	*Just a minute. Don't go. Can you tell me where I can eat near here?*
Botones	¿Prefiere comida norteamericana o mexicana?	*Do you prefer American food or Mexican food?*
Thomas	Me gustaría comer algo mexicano.	*I'd like to eat something Mexican.*
Botones	Hay un restaurante bastante bueno al otro lado de la calle. Se llama "El Tampiqueño".	*There's a fairly good restaurant right across the street. It's called El Tampiqueño.*
Thomas	Muchas gracias. Aquí tiene.	*Thanks a lot. Here you are.*

Asking for Directions
Story

Johnny	Creo que nos hemos perdido.	*I think we're lost.*
Susy	Perdone, señora, ¿puede decirme dónde está la oficina de correos?	*Excuse me, ma'am. Can you tell me where the post office is?*
Señora	No está muy lejos. Está en la calle Bolívar.	*It's not far from here. It's on Bolívar Street.*
Susy	¿Cómo podemos llegar hasta allá?	*How can we get there from here?*
Señora	Siga todo derecho hasta la calle Nogales.	*Go straight until you get to Nogales Street.*

continued...

Asking for Directions
Story: continued

Señora	Entonces, doble a la izquierda y camine dos cuadras hasta la calle Bolívar. Verá usted la oficina en la esquina.	*Then, turn left and walk two blocks to Bolívar Street. You'll see the post office on the corner.*
Johnny	¿Y sabe usted a qué hora se cierra la oficina?	*And do you know what time the office closes?*
Señora	Creo que se cierra a las cuatro de la tarde.	*I think it closes at four p.m.*
Susy	Muy amable. Gracias.	*You've been very kind. Thank you.*
Señora	De nada.	*You're welcome.*

Action

Thomas	Perdone, señora, ¿puede decirme dónde está la oficina de correos?	*Excuse me, ma'am. Can you tell me where the post office is?*
Señora	No está muy lejos. Está en la calle Bolívar.	*It's not far from here. It's on Bolívar Street.*
Thomas	¿Cómo puedo llegar hasta allá?	*How can I get there from here?*
Señora	Siga todo derecho hasta la calle Nogales.	*Go straight until you get to Nogales Street.*
Señora	Entonces, doble a la izquierda y camine dos cuadras hasta la calle Bolívar. Verá usted la oficina en la esquina.	*Then, turn left and walk two blocks to Bolívar Street. You'll see the post office on the corner.*
Thomas	¿Y sabe usted a qué hora se cierra la oficina?	*And do you know what time the office closes?*
Señora	Creo que se cierra a las cuatro de la tarde.	*I think it closes at four p.m.*
Thomas	Muy amable. Gracias.	*You've been very kind. Thank you.*
Señora	De nada.	*You're welcome.*

Planning a Trip
Story

Roberto	La verdad es que no me apetece manejar. Creo que es mejor tomar el autobús.	*The truth is I don't feel like driving. I think it's better to take a bus.*
Silvia	¿Tú quieres ir con un tour organizado?	*Do you want to go on a tour?*
Roberto	Sí, porque así no tendremos que preocuparnos de nada.	*Yes, because then we won't have to worry about anything.*
Silvia	Eduardo me dijo que algunas de estas excurciones son muy interesantes.	*Eduardo told me that some of these trips are really interesting.*
Roberto	¿Adónde vamos? ¿Al mar o a las montañas?	*Where will we go? To the sea or to the mountains?*
Silvia	Me dijeron que el viaje a Acapulco es muy agradable porque pasamos por Taxco, una ciudad colonial, y por las montañas también.	*They told me that the trip to Acapulco is nice because we go through Taxco, a colonial city, and through the mountains too.*
Roberto	¿Vamos a quedarnos algunos días en la playa? A mi me gustaría ponerme moreno.	*Are we going to spend a few days at the beach? I'd like to get a tan.*
Silvia	Sí, por supuesto. También podemos recorrer la costa para poder conocer algunos pueblos pequeños.	*Yes, of course. We can also travel along the coast in order to see some of the small towns.*
Roberto	De acuerdo. Mañana puedo ir a la agencia de viajes para decirles que queremos hacer un viaje a Acapulco.	*O.K. Tomorrow I can go to the travel agency and tell them we want to take a trip to Acapulco.*

Action

| Thomas | La verdad es que no me apetece manejar. Creo que es mejor tomar el autobús. | *The truth is I don't feel like driving. I think it's better to take a bus.* |
| Elena | ¿Tú quieres ir con un tour organizado? | *Do you want to go on a tour?* |

continued...

Planning a Trip
Action: continued

Thomas	Sí, porque así no tendremos que preocuparnos de nada.	*Yes, because then we won't have to worry about anything.*
Thomas	Roberto me dijo que algunas de estas excursiones son muy interesantes.	*Roberto told me that some of these trips are really interesting.*
Elena	¿Adónde vamos? ¿Al mar o a las montañas?	*Where will we go? To the sea or to the mountains?*
Thomas	Me dijeron que el viaje a Acapulco es agradable porque pasamos por Taxco, una ciudad colonial, y las montañas también.	*They told me that the trip to Acapulco is nice because we go through Taxco, a colonial city, and through the mountains too.*
Elena	¿Vamos a quedarnos algunos días en la playa? A mí me gustaría ponerme morena.	*Are we going to spend a few days at the beach? I'd like to get a tan.*
Thomas	Sí, por supuesto. También podemos recorrer la costa para poder conocer algunos pueblos pequeños.	*Yes, of course. We can also travel along the coast in order to see some of the small towns.*

Making Travel Reservations
Story

Roberto	Buenos días. Mi esposa y yo queremos ir de vacaciones a Acapulco con un tour.	*Good morning. My wife and I want to go on an organized tour to Acapulco for vacation.*
Roberto	¿Puede darme información sobre los viajes?	*Can you give me some information about the trip?*
Agente	Sí, señor. Tenemos varias clases de excursiones. ¿Quieren ir en primera clase?	*Yes, Sir. We have several different kinds of tours. Do you want to go first class?*
Roberto	Sí, y quiero reservar dos plazas.	*Yes, and I want to reserve two places.*
Agente	¿Cuándo quieren viajar?	*When do you want to travel?*

continued...

Making Travel Reservations
Story: continued

Roberto	Tenemos una semana libre, a partir del viernes próximo.	*We have a week free, starting next Friday.*
Agente	Bueno. Pueden salir ustedes el sábado por la mañana y llegar a Taxco por la noche.	*Fine. You can leave on Saturday morning and get to Taxco that night.*
Agente	La excursión incluye alojamiento en Taxco, cena y desayuno, y por la noche pueden asistir a una representación folklórica.	*The tour includes hotel accommodations in Taxco, dinner and breakfast, and in the evening you can attend a floor show of folkloric dances.*
Roberto	Me parece estupendo.	*It sounds great to me.*
Roberto	¿Habrá tiempo para visitar las tiendas?	*Will there be time to visit the stores?*
Agente	Sí, tendrán un par de horas antes de salir para Acapulco.	*Yes, you'll have a couple of hours before you leave for Acapulco.*

Action

Elena	Buenos días. Mi familia y yo queremos ir de vacaciones a Acapulco con un tour.	*Good morning. My family and I want to go on an organized tour to Acapulco for vacation.*
Elena	¿Puede darme información sobre los viajes?	*Can you give me some information about the trips?*
Agente	Sí, señora. Tenemos varias clases de excursiones. ¿Quieren ir en primera clase?	*Yes, Ma'am. We have several different kinds of tours. Do you want to go first class?*
Elena	Sí, y quiero reservar cuatro plazas. Tenemos una semana libre, a partir del viernes próximo.	*Yes, and I want to reserve four places. We have a week free, starting next Friday.*
Agente	Bueno. Pueden salir ustedes el sábado por la mañana y llegar a Taxco por la noche.	*Fine. You can leave on Saturday morning and get to Taxco that night.*

continued...

Making Travel Reservations
Action: continued

Agente	La excursión incluye alojamiento en Taxco, cena y desayuno, y por la noche pueden asistir a una representación folklórica.	*The tour includes hotel accommodations in Taxco, dinner and breakfast, and in the evening you can attend a floor show of folkloric dances.*
Elena	Me parece estupendo. ¿Habrá tiempo para visitar las tiendas?	*It sounds great to me. Will there be time to visit the stores?*
Agente	Sí, tendrán un par de horas antes de salir para Acapulco.	*Yes, you'll have a couple of hours before you leave for Acapulco.*

Going to Lunch
Story

Camarero	Buenas tardes. ¿Espera usted a alguien?	*Good afternoon. Are you waiting for someone?*
Eduardo	No, estoy solo.	*No, I'm alone.*
Camarero	¿Dónde quiere sentarse?	*Where do you want to sit?*
Eduardo	Cerca de la ventana, por favor.	*Near the window, please.*
Camarero	¿Desea tomar algo antes de pedir?	*Do you want something to drink before you order?*
Eduardo	Sí, tráigame una cerveza fría, por favor.	*Yes, bring me a cold beer.*
Camarero	¿Qué desea comer?	*What do you want to eat?*
Eduardo	Quiero un consomé de pollo, las enchiladas suizas y una ensalada verde.	*I want chicken soup, enchiladas suizas, and a green salad.*
Camarero	Muy bien.	*Very well.*
Camarero	Qué disfrute su almuerzo.	*Enjoy your lunch.*
Eduardo	Gracias.	*Thank you.*
Camarero	¿Quiere tomar algo de postre?	*Would you like something for dessert?*
Eduardo	No gracias. Tráigame la cuenta, por favor.	*No thanks. Bring me the bill, please.*

Going to Lunch
Action

Camarero	Buenas noches. ¿Espera usted a alguien?	*Good evening. Are you waiting for someone?*
Thomas	No, estoy solo.	*No, I'm alone.*
Camarero	¿Dónde quiere sentarse?	*Where do you want to sit?*
Thomas	Cerca de la ventana, por favor.	*Near the window, please.*
Camarero	¿Desea tomar algo antes de pedir?	*Do you want something to drink before you order?*
Thomas	Sí, tráigame una cerveza fría.	*Yes, bring me a cold beer.*
Camarero	¿Qué desea comer?	*What do you want to eat?*
Thomas	Quiero un consomé de pollo, las enchiladas suizas y una ensalada verde.	*I want chicken soup, enchiladas suizas, and a green salad.*
Camarero	Muy bien.	*Very well.*
Camarero	¿Quiere tomar algo de postre?	*Would you like something for dessert?*
Thomas	No gracias. Tráigame la cuenta, por favor.	*No thanks. Bring me the bill, please.*

Buying Presents
Story

Roberto	¿Qué te parece este pañuelo para Karen?	*What do you think about this scarf for Karen?*
Silvia	Creo que los colores son muy chillones.	*I think the colors are too loud.*
Silvia	¿No quieres buscar algo más discreto?	*Don't you want to look for something more subtle?*
Roberto	Tienes razón. Creo que aquel azul es más discreto.	*You're right. I think that blue one over there is more subtle.*
Silvia	¿Qué podemos comprarle a Mario?	*What can we buy for Mario?*
Roberto	A Mario le encanta la música clásica. Cómprale un disco.	*Mario loves classical music. Buy him a record.*

continued...

Buying Presents
Story: continued

Silvia	Tenemos que comprarles unos juguetes a los niños también.	*We have to buy some toys for the children too.*
Silvia	Voy a preguntar a la dependienta dónde está la sección de juguetes.	*I'm going to ask the saleswoman where the toy section is.*
Roberto	No te olvides del libro para Eduardo.	*Don't forget the book for Eduardo.*
Roberto	Tienen una buena selección ahí, junto a la caja.	*They have a good selection there, next to the cash register.*
Silvia	No, prefiero ir a la librería. Allá los libros son más baratos que aquí.	*No, I prefer to go to the bookstore. There, the books are cheaper than here.*

Action

Elena	¿Qué te parece este pañuelo para Silvia?	*What do you think about this scarf for Silvia?*
Thomas	Creo que los colores son muy chillones. ¿No quieres buscar algo más discreto?	*I think the colors are too loud. Don't you want to look for something more subtle?*
Elena	Tienes razón. Creo que aquel azul es más elegante.	*You're right. I think that blue one over there is more elegant.*
Thomas	¿Qué podemos comprarle a Roberto?	*And what can we buy for Roberto?*
Elena	A Roberto le encanta la música clásica. Cómprale un disco.	*Roberto loves classical music. Buy him a record.*
Thomas	Tenemos que comprarles unos juguetes a los niños, también.	*We have to buy some toys for the children too.*
Elena	No te olvides del libro para Eduardo. Tienen una buena selección ahí, junto a la caja.	*Don't forget the book for Eduardo. They have a good selection there, next to the cash register.*
Thomas	No, prefiero ir a la librería. Allá los libros son más baratos que aquí.	*No, I prefer to go to the bookstore. There, the books are cheaper than here.*
Thomas	Voy a preguntar a la dependienta dónde está la sección de juguetes.	*I'm going to ask the saleswoman where the toy section is.*

At the Airport
Story

Karen	¿Hay demora con el vuelo para Chicago?	*Is there a delay on the flight to Chicago?*
Empleado	No. Saldrá a las 11:45 desde la puerta 16.	*No. It'll leave at 11:45, from gate 16.*
Empleado	¿Quieren documentar el equipaje ahora?	*Do you want to check your baggage now?*
Mario	Sí. llevamos muchas maletas.	*Yes. We're carrying a lot of luggage.*
Empleado	¿Tiene los pasajes?	*Do you have your tickets?*
Karen	Sí, claro. Aquí tiene.	*Yes, of course. Here they are.*
Empleado	Gracias. Pidieron asientos en la sección de no fumar, ¿verdad?	*Thank you. You asked for seats in the no smoking section, right?*
Karen	Sí.	*Yes.*
Mario	¿Con cuánto tiempo de antelación tenemos que estar aquí?	*How far in advance do we need to be here?*
Empleado	Veinte minutos antes del embarque. Anunciarán la salida en la sala de espera.	*Twenty minutes before boarding. They'll announce the departure in the waiting room.*
Karen	No puedo creer que es hora de salir, Mario.	*I can't believe that it's time to leave, Mario.*
Karen	Después de pasar un año tan agradable en México, hay que regresar a Chicago.	*After spending a very enjoyable year here in Mexico, it's necessary to return to Chicago.*
Mario	Tampoco lo creo. Pero si no me equivoco, tenemos tres semanas libres en julio, y si economizamos un poco, ¡podremos venir a México de vacaciones!	*I don't believe it either. But, if I'm not mistaken, we have three weeks off in July, and if we save a little, we'll be able to return to Mexico on vacation!*

At the Airport
Action

Thomas	¿Hay demora con el vuelo para Chicago?	*Is there a delay on the flight to Chicago?*
Empleado	No. Saldrá a las 11:45 desde la puerta 16. ¿Quieren documentar el equipaje ahora?	*No. It'll leave at 11:45, from gate 16. Do you want to check your baggage now?*
Thomas	Sí. Llevamos muchas maletas.	*Yes. We're carrying a lot of luggage.*
Empleado	¿Tiene los pasajes?	*Do you have your tickets?*
Elena	Sí, claro. Aquí tiene.	*Yes, of course. Here they are.*
Empleado	Gracias. Pidieron asientos en la sección de no fumar, ¿verdad?	*Thank you. You asked for seats in the no smoking section, right?*
Elena	Sí. ¿Con cuánto tiempo de antelación tenemos que estar aquí?	*Yes. How far in advance do we need to be here?*
Empleado	Veinte minutos antes del embarque. Anunciarán la salida en la sala de espera.	*Twenty minutes before boarding. They'll announce the departure in the waiting room.*
Elena	No puedo creer que es hora de salir, Thomas. Después de pasar un año tan agradable aquí en México, hay que regresar a Chicago.	*I can't believe that it's time to leave, Thomas. After spending a very enjoyable year here in Mexico, it's necessary to return to Chicago.*
Thomas	Tampoco lo creo. Pero, si no me equivoco, tengo tres semanas libres en julio, y si economizamos un poco, ¡podremos venir a México de vacaciones!	*I don't believe it either. But, if I'm not mistaken, I have three weeks off in July, and if we save a little, we'll be able to return to Mexico on vacation!*

BUSINESS
Making a Long Distance Phone Call
Story

Operadora	¿Bueno?	*Hello?*
Susy	Quiero hacer una llamada a Estados Unidos, por favor.	*I want to make a call to the United States, please.*
Operadora	¿De persona a persona?	*Person to person?*
Susy	Sí, con la señora Ana Santiago, por cobrar, por favor.	*Yes, with Mrs. Ana Santiago, collect, please.*
Operadora	Y ¿cómo se llama usted?	*And what is your name?*
Susy	Susy, Susy Santiago.	*Susy, Susy Santiago.*
Operadora	¿El número, por favor?	*The number, please?*
Susy	Es el 423-450-2105.	*It's 423-450-2105.*
Operadora	Ahora mismo.	*Right away.*
Operadora	Lo siento, no contesta nadie. ¿Quiere que insista?	*I'm sorry. No one answers. Do you want me to keep trying?*
Susy	Sí, por favor.	*Yes, please.*
Operadora	Todavía no contesta nadie. ¿Quiere volver a llamar más tarde?	*There's still no answer. Would you like to call back later?*
Susy	Está bien. Llamaré más tarde. Gracias.	*Alright. I'll call later. Thanks.*
Operadora	No hay de que. Adiós.	*Don't mention it. Good-bye.*
Susy	Adiós.	*Good-bye.*

Action

Thomas	Quiero hacer una llamada a Estados Unidos, por favor.	*I want to make a call to the United States, please.*
Operadora	¿Por cobrar?	*Do you want to reverse the charges?*
Thomas	Sí.	*Yes.*
Operadora	¿El número, por favor?	*What's the number, please?*
Thomas	Es el 615-974-2311. De persona a persona, con la señora Elena Smith.	*It's 615-974-2311. Person to person, to Mrs. Elena Smith.*

continued...

Making a Long Distance Phone Call
Action: continued

Operadora	Ahora mismo.	*Right away.*
Operadora	Lo siento. No contesta nadie. ¿Quiere que insista?	*I'm sorry. No one answers. Do you want me to keep trying?*
Thomas	No, gracias. Llamaré más tarde.	*No, thanks. I'll call later.*

Making a Local Phone Call
Story

Mario	¿Puede decirme cómo llamar directamente dentro de la ciudad?	*Can you tell me how to make a local phone call?*
Operadora	Sí, señor. Marque el número seis primero, y después el número que usted desee.	*Yes, sir. Dial number 6 first, then the number that you want.*
Secretaria	Bueno.	*Hello.*
Mario	¿Está la señora Garcia?	*Is Mrs. García in?*
Secretaria	¿De parte de quién?	*Who's calling, please?*
Mario	De parte de Mario Santiago.	*Mario Santiago.*
Secretaria	Lo siento. La señora Garcia no está en su oficina; está en una reunión.	*I'm sorry. Mrs. García is in a meeting.*
Secretaria	¿Quiere dejar un recado?	*Do you want to leave a message?*
Mario	Sí, dígale que me llame al Hotel Internacional.	*Yes, tell her to call me at the Hotel Internacional.*
Mario	Estoy aquí hasta las nueve.	*I'll be here until nine.*
Secretaria	¡Cómo no! ¿Algo más?	*Of course. Anything else?*
Mario	Nada más, gracias. Adiós.	*That's all, thanks. Good-bye.*
Secretaria	Muy bien. Adiós.	*Alright. Good-bye.*

Making a Local Phone Call
Action

Thomas	¿Puede decirme cómo llamar directamente dentro de la ciudad?	*Can you tell me how to make a local phone call?*
Operadora	Sí, señor. Marque el número 6 primero, y después el número que usted desee.	*Yes, sir. Dial number 6 first, then the number that you want.*
Thomas	Gracias.	*Thanks.*
Thomas	¿Está el señor García?	*Is Mr. García in?*
Secretaria	¿De parte de quién?	*Who's calling, please?*
Thomas	De parte de Thomas Smith.	*Thomas Smith.*
Secretaria	Lo siento. El señor García está en una reunión. ¿Quiere dejar un recado?	*I'm sorry. Mr. García is in a meeting. Do you want to leave a message?*
Thomas	Sí, dígale que me llame al Hotel Internacional. Estoy aquí hasta las nueve.	*Yes, tell him to call me at the Hotel Internacional. I'll be here until nine.*
Secretaria	¡Cómo no! ¿Algo más?	*Of course. Anything else?*
Thomas	Nada más, gracias. Adiós.	*That's all, thanks. Good-bye.*

Going to Dinner
Story

Silvia	¿Dónde está la carne en este restaurante?	*Don't they have any meat in this restaurant?*
Roberto	¿Pero no querías comer pescado?	*But didn't you want to eat seafood?*
Silvia	Quería, pero ahora quiero comer carne.	*I did want to, but now I want to eat meat.*
Roberto	Pues vas a tener que preguntarle al camarero.	*Well you'll have to ask the waiter.*
Silvia	¿Es posible comer un bistec con papas fritas? Es que no me apetece comer pescado hoy.	*Is it possible to get a steak and fried potatoes? I just don't feel like eating fish today.*
Camarero	Por supuesto. Hablaré con el cocinero.	*Of course. I'll talk to the chef.*

continued...

Going to Dinner
Story: continued

Camarero	Y usted, señor, ¿qué va a tomar?	*And you, sir, what will you have to eat?*
Roberto	¿Tienen alguna especialidad?	*Do you have any specialities of the house?*
Camarero	Sí, camarones, langosta y atún.	*Yes, shrimp, lobster and tuna.*
Roberto	La langosta para mí.	*Lobster for me.*
Camarero	¿Algo de beber?	*Anything to drink?*
Silvia	Sí, vino, por favor.	*Yes, some wine, please.*

Action

Thomas	¿Dónde está la carne en este restaurante?	*Don't they have any meat in this restaurant?*
Elena	¿Pero no querías comer pescado?	*But didn't you want to eat seafood?*
Thomas	Quería, pero ahora quiero comer carne.	*I did want to, but now I want to eat meat.*
Elena	Pues vas a tener que preguntarle al camarero.	*Well you'll have to ask the waiter.*
Thomas	¿Es posible comer un bistec con papas fritas? Es que no me apetece comer pescado hoy.	*Is it possible to get a steak and fried potatoes? I just don't feel like eating fish today.*
Camarero	Por supuesto. Hablaré con el cocinero. Y la señora y los niños, ¿qué van a tomar?	*Of course. I'll talk to the chef. And the lady and the children, what will they have to eat?*
Elena	¿Tienen alguna especialidad?	*Do you have any specialities of the house?*
Camarero	Sí, camarones, langosta y atún.	*Yes, shrimp, lobster and tuna.*
Elena	La langosta para mí. Los niños son como su padre. Prefieren la carne.	*Lobster for me. And the children are like their father. They prefer meat.*
Camarero	¿Algo de beber?	*Anything to drink?*
Thomas	Vino para nosotros y jugo para los niños.	*Wine for us, and juice for the children.*

Finding an Office
Story

Karen	¿Puede indicarme dónde queda la oficina de la señora González?	*Can you tell me where Mrs. González's office is?*
Recepcionista	Está en el tercer piso, al final del pasillo a la derecha.	*It's on the third floor, at the end of the hall on the right.*
Recepcionista	El ascensor está a su izquierda.	*The elevator is on your left.*
Karen	Gracias, pero prefiero subir andando.	*Thanks, but I prefer to walk up.*
Karen	¿Dónde quedan las escaleras?	*Where are the stairs?*
Recepcionista	Detrás de usted.	*Behind you.*
Karen	¿Está la señora González?	*Is Mrs. González here?*
Secretaria	No. Se ha equivocado de puerta.	*No. You've made a mistake.*
Secretaria	Sí usted busca a la señora González, tiene que llamar en la puerta siguiente.	*If you're looking for Mr. González, you have to go next door.*
Karen	¿Es ésta la oficina de la señora González?	*Is this Mrs. González's office?*
Secretaria	Sí. ¿Es usted la señora Santiago?	*Yes. Are you Mrs. Santiago?*
Karen	Sí. Soy Karen Santiago.	*Yes. I'm Karen Santiago.*
Secretaria	Pase. La señora González la está esperando.	*Come in. Mrs. González is waiting for you.*

Action

Thomas	¿Puede indicarme dónde queda la oficina de la señora González?	*Can you tell me where Mrs. González's office is?*
Recepcionista	Está en el tercer piso, al final del pasillo a la derecha. El ascensor está a su izquierda.	*It's on the third floor, at the end of the hall on the right. The elevator is on your left.*
Thomas	Gracias, pero prefiero subir andando. ¿Dónde están las escaleras?	*Thanks, but I prefer to walk up. Where are the stairs?*
Recepcionista	Detrás de usted.	*Behind you.*

continued...

Finding an Office
Action: continued

Thomas	¿Está el Sr. González?	*Is Mr. González here?*
Secretaria	No. Se ha equivocado de puerta. Tiene que llamar en la puerta siguiente.	*No. You've made a mistake. You have to go next door.*
Thomas	¿Es ésta la oficina del Sr. González?	*Is this Mr. González's office?*
Secretaria	Sí. ¿Es usted el Sr. Smith? Pase. El Sr. González lo está esperando.	*Yes. Are you Mr. Smith? Come in. Mr. González is waiting for you.*

Greetings and Introductions
Story

Silvia	Hola, Karen. ¿Cómo estás?	*Hello, Karen. How are you?*
Karen	Bien, gracias. Y tú, ¿qué tal estás?	*Just fine, thanks. And you, how are you doing?*
Silvia	Ya ves. Trabajando como siempre.	*As you can see. Working like always.*
Silvia	¿Qué tal el viaje?	*How was your trip?*
Karen	Muy bien, gracias.	*Very nice, thanks.*
Silvia	¿Conoces a mi socio, Eduardo González?	*Do you know my partner, Eduardo González?*
Karen	Encantada de conocerlo.	*I'm glad to meet you.*
Eduardo	Igualmente. Silvia me dice que va a trabajar con nosotros. Me alegro.	*The pleasure's mine. Silvia tells me you're going to work with us. I'm pleased.*
Karen	Pues sí, mi intención es quedarme aquí un año por lo menos.	*Well, yes, my intention is to stay here for at least a year.*
Silvia	¿Vas a traer a tu familia?	*Are you going to have your family join you?*
Karen	Claro. Están aquí.	*Of course. They are here.*
Karen	Ahora solo tenemos que encontrar un apartamento.	*Now we just have to find an apartment.*
Silvia	Si quieres, puedo acompañarte a la inmobiliaria.	*If you want, I can go with you to the rental agency.*

Greetings and Introductions
Action

Roberto	Hola, Thomas. ¿Cómo estás? ¿Qué tal el viaje?	*Hello, Thomas. How are you? How was your trip?*
Thomas	Muy bien, gracias. Y tú, ¿qué tal estás?	*Just fine, thanks. And you, how are you doing?*
Roberto	Ya ves. Trabajando, como siempre. ¿Conoces a mi socio, Eduardo Gutiérrez?	*As you can see. Working like always. Do you know my partner, Eduardo Gutiérrez?*
Thomas	Encantado de conocerlo.	*I'm glad to meet you.*
Eduardo	Igualmente. Roberto me dice que usted va a trabajar con nosotros. Me alegro.	*The pleasure's mine. Roberto tells me you're going to work with us. I'm pleased.*
Thomas	Pues sí, mi intención es quedarme aquí un año por lo menos.	*Well, yes, my intention is to stay here for at least a year.*
Roberto	¿Vas a traer a tu mujer?	*Are you going to have your wife join you?*
Thomas	Claro. Elena tiene ganas de venir, pero primero tengo que encontrar un apartamento.	*Of course. Elena wants to come, but first I have to find an apartment.*
Eduardo	Tengo tiempo libre el viernes. Si quiere, puedo acompañarlo a la inmobiliaria.	*I have some free time on Friday. If you want, I can go with you to the rental agency.*

Making an Appointment
Story

Mario	¿Podemos vernos mañana por la mañana?	*Can we meet tomorrow morning?*
Eduardo	¿A qué hora le conviene a usted?	*What's a convenient time for you?*
Mario	¿Entre las diez y las once?	*Between ten and eleven?*
Eduardo	Es un poco difícil para mí.	*That's a little difficult for me.*
Eduardo	¿Qué le parece el martes por la tarde? ¿Le parece bien a las cuatro?	*What about Tuesday in the afternoon? Would four o'clock be alright?*

continued...

Making an Appointment
Story: continued

Mario	El martes me parece un buen día, pero tengo que ir a Cuernavaca por la mañana.	*Tuesday is a good day for me, but I have to go to Cuernavaca in the morning.*
Mario	Trataré de estar aquí de vuelta antes de las cuatro.	*I'll try to be back here before four.*
Mario	Depende del tráfico. Usted sabe el problema que hay a esa hora.	*It depends on the traffic. You know what problems there are at that time.*
Eduardo	Sí, comprendo. Los embotellamientos son terribles a veces.	*Yes, I understand. The traffic jams are horrible sometimes.*
Eduardo	No se preocupe si llega un poco más tarde. Voy a estar en mi oficina hasta las seis.	*Don't worry if you get here a bit late. I'm going to be at the office until six.*
Mario	Podemos tomar una copa a esa hora y hablar del tema, si le parece.	*We could have a drink then and talk about the matter, if that sounds alright to you.*
Eduardo	Es una buena idea.	*That's a good idea.*
Eduardo	Nos vemos entonces.	*We'll see each other then.*
Mario	Hasta luego.	*See you then.*

Action

Thomas	¿Podemos vernos mañana por la mañana?	*Can we meet tomorrow morning?*
Cliente	¿A qué hora le conviene a usted?	*What's a convenient time for you?*
Thomas	¿Entre las diez y las once?	*Between ten and eleven?*
Cliente	Es un poco difícil para mí. ¿Qué le parece el martes por la tarde? ¿Le parece bien a las cuatro?	*That's a little difficult for me. What about Tuesday in the afternoon? Would four o'clock be alright?*
Thomas	El martes me parece un buen día, pero tengo que ir a Cuernavaca por la mañana.	*Tuesday is a good day for me, but I have to go to Cuernavaca in the morning.*

continued...

Making an Appointment
Action: continued

Thomas	Trataré de estar aquí de vuelta antes de las cuatro.	*I'll try to be back here before four.*
Thomas	Depende del tráfico. Usted sabe el problema que hay a esa hora.	*It depends on the traffic. You know what problems there are at that time.*
Cliente	Sí, comprendo. Los embotellamientos son terribles a veces.	*Yes, I understand. The traffic jams are horrible sometimes.*
Cliente	No se preocupe si llega un poco más tarde. Voy a estar en mi oficina hasta las seis.	*Don't worry if you get here a bit late. I'm going to be at the office until six.*
Cliente	Podemos tomar una copa a esa hora y hablar del tema, si le parece.	*We could have a drink then and talk about the matter, if that sounds alright to you.*
Thomas	Es una buena idea. Nos vemos entonces.	*That's a good idea. We'll see each other then.*

Banking
Story

Karen	¿Ha llegado una transferencia desde Estados Unidos a nombre de Karen Santiago?	*Has some money arrived from the United States in the name of Karen Santiago?*
Empleado	¿Tiene usted una cuenta aquí?	*Do you have an account here?*
Karen	Sí, abrí una cuenta hace un mes.	*Yes, I opened an account a month ago.*
Empleado	¿Cuál es el número?	*What is the number?*
Karen	Lo tengo aquí. Es el C-4400761.	*I have it here. It's C-4400761.*
Empleado	Espere un momento. Sí, en efecto. Tiene usted una cuenta con un balance de veinte mil pesos.	*Wait a minute. Yes, that's right. You have an account with a balance of twenty thousand pesos.*

continued...

Banking
Story: continued

Karen	Estupendo. Quiero encargar unos cheques de viaje. Cinco mil pesos, pero en sucres, si es posible.	*Great. I want to get some traveler's checks. Five thousand pesos, but in sucres, if that's possible.*
Empleado	Estarán mañana por la mañana a última hora.	*They'll be ready late tomorrow morning.*
Empleado	¿Desea algo más?	*Do you want anything else?*
Karen	No, es todo, gracias. Hasta luego.	*No, that's all, thanks. See you later.*

Action

Thomas	¿Ha llegado una transferencia desde Estados Unidos a nombre de Thomas Smith?	*Has some money arrived from the United States in the name of Thomas Smith?*
Empleado	¿Tiene usted una cuenta aquí?	*Do you have an account here?*
Thomas	Sí, abrí una cuenta hace un mes.	*Yes, I opened an account a month ago.*
Empleado	¿Cuál es el número?	*What is the number?*
Thomas	Lo tengo aquí. Es el C-4400761.	*I have it here. It's C-4400761.*
Empleado	Espere un momento. Sí, en efecto. Tiene usted una cuenta con un balance de veinte mil pesos.	*Wait a minute. Yes, that's right. You have an account with a balance of twenty thousand pesos.*
Thomas	Estupendo. Quiero encargar unos cheques de viaje. Cinco mil pesos, pero en sucres, de ser posible.	*Great. I want to get some traveler's checks. Five thousand pesos, but in sucres, if that's possible.*
Empleado	Estarán mañana por la mañana a última hora. ¿Desea algo más?	*They'll be ready late tomorrow morning. Do you want anything else?*
Thomas	No, es todo, gracias. Hasta luego.	*No, that's all, thanks. See you later.*

Planning an Evening Out
Story

Roberto	¿Tiene usted algún plan para el viernes en la noche?	*Do you have plans for Friday night?*
Karen	No. Espero que terminemos el trabajo y asi tendré dos dias para ver la ciudad.	*No. I hope that we'll finish the job and then I'll have two days to see the city.*
Roberto	Hay una representación de teatro en Bellas Artes y pensé que quizás le gustaria acompañarnos.	*There's a play at the Bellas Artes theater and I thought that perhaps you'd like to accompany us.*
Karen	¿No es un poco tarde para conseguir boletos?	*Isn't it a little late to get tickets?*
Roberto	No, no se preocupe. Estoy seguro que quedan entradas.	*No, don't worry. I'm sure there are tickets left.*
Karen	Por cierto, ¿a qué hora es la función?	*By the way, at what time is the performance?*
Roberto	Es a las nueve. Pero vamos a cenar en un restaurante antes.	*At nine. But we're going to have dinner in a restaurant beforehand.*
Karen	Ay, ya Eduardo nos invitó a cenar en su casa.	*Ah, Eduardo alredy invited us to have dinner at his house.*
Roberto	¡Qué lástima! Quizás en otra ocasión, entonces.	*What a shame! Maybe some other time, then.*
Karen	Pero si nos gustaria acompañarles al teatro.	*But we would like to join you at the theatre.*
Karen	¿Podía usted pasar a recogernos en el apartamento a las ocho?	*can you come to pick us up at the apartment at eight?*
Roberto	No hay ningún problema.	*No problem.*

Action

Thomas	¿Tiene usted algún plan para el viernes en la noche?	*Do you have plans for Friday night?*
Directora	No. Espero que terminemos el trabajo y asi tendré dos dias para ver la ciudad.	*No. I hope that we'll finish the job and then I'll have two days to see the city.*

continued...

Planning an Evening Out
Action: continued

Thomas	Hay una representación de teatro en Bellas Artes y pensé que quizás le gustaria acompañarnos.	*There's a play at the Bellas Artes theater and I thought that perhaps you'd like to accompany us.*
Directora	¿No es un poco tarde para conseguir boletos?	*Isn't it a little late to get tickets?*
Thomas	No, no se preocupe. Estoy seguro que quedan entradas.	*No, don't worry. I'm sure there are tickets left.*
Directora	Por cierto, ¿a qué hora es la función?	*By the way, at what time is the performance?*
Thomas	A las nueve.	*At nine.*
Directora	Muy bien. ¿Podría usted pasar a recogerme en mi hotel a las ocho?	*Can you come to pick me up at my hotel at eight?*
Thomas	No hay ningún problema.	*No problem.*

EVERYDAY LIFE
At a Party
Story

Silvia	¡Hola, Karen, encantada de verte, Mario! Pasen.	*Hi, Karen, happy to see you, Mario! Come in.*
Silvia	¿Cómo están los niños?	*How are the children?*
Karen	Están bien, gracias.	*They're fine, thanks.*
Roberto	¿Mario y Karen, cómo están?	*Mario and Karen, how are you?*
Mario	Bien, gracias, Roberto.	*Fine, thanks, Roberto.*
Mario	Estupendo volver a verte.	*It's great to see you again.*
Silvia	¿Conoces a todos los invitados?	*Do you know all the guests?*
Karen	A algunos. ¿Quién es la mujer que baila con Roberto?	*Some of them. And, who's the woman dancing with Roberto?*
Silvia	Es mi hermana menor. Vive en Mérida, pero está aquí de visita un par de días.	*She's my younger sister. She lives in Mérida, but she's here visiting for a couple of days.*
Karen	Y ¿quién es el que está en el balcón conversando con Eduardo?	*And, who is the man on the balcony talking to Eduardo?*
Silvia	Es su primo. Es abogado y también da clases en la universidad.	*It's his cousin. He's a lawyer and he also teaches at the university.*
Karen	Parece que la fiesta está muy animada.	*It looks like the party's very lively.*

Action

Silvia	¡Encantada de verte, Thomas! Pasa. ¿Cómo está la familia? ¿Cuándo va a venir Elena?	*Happy to see you, Thomas! Come in. How's your family? When is Elena coming?*
Thomas	Están todos bien, gracias. Elena viene dentro de dos semanas y traerá a los niños.	*They're all fine, thanks. Elena is coming within the next two weeks and she brings the children with her.*
Silvia	Será estupendo volver a verlos. ¿Conoces a todos los invitados?	*It'll be great to see them again. Do you know all the guests?*

continued...

At a Party
Action: continued

Thomas	A algunos. Y ¿quién es la mujer que está bailando con Roberto?	*Some of them. And, who's the woman dancing with Roberto?*
Silvia	Es mi hermana menor. Vive en Mérida, pero está aquí de visita un par de días.	*She's my younger sister. She lives in Mérida, but she's here visiting for a couple of days.*
Thomas	Y ¿quién es el que está en el balcón conversando con Eduardo?	*And, who is the man on the balcony talking to Eduardo?*
Silvia	Es su primo. Es abogado y también da clases en la universidad.	*It's his cousin. He's a lawyer and he also teaches at the university.*
Thomas	Parece que la fiesta está muy animada.	*It looks like the party's very lively.*

Going to a Pharmacy
Story

Karen	¿Tiene algo para el dolor de estómago?	*Do you have something for a stomachache?*
Farmacéutico	¿Qué le ocurre?	*What's wrong with you?*
Karen	No lo sé. Comí algo anoche y no me siento muy bien.	*I don't know. I ate something last night and I don't feel very well.*
Farmacéutico	¿Tiene fiebre, diarrea o náuseas? ¿O es un dolor agudo?	*Do you have diarrhea or are you nauseous? Or is it a sharp pain?*
Karen	Es más bien un malestar general.	*I just don't feel well in general.*
Farmacéutico	¿Consultó a un médico?	*Did you see a doctor?*
Karen	Todavía no. ¿Necesito una receta?	*Not yet. Do I need a prescription?*
Farmacéutico	Para estas pastillas no, pero si usted se siente mal mañana, le aconsejo que vea a un médico.	*For these pills, no, but if you still feel ill tomorrow, I recommend you see a doctor.*
Karen	Primero voy a ver si estas pastillas me ayudan.	*First I'll see if these pills help me.*
Farmacéutico	Tome dos cada cuatro horas.	*Take two every four hours.*
Farmacéutico	Espero que se mejore.	*I hope you feel better.*

Going to a Pharmacy
Action

Thomas	¿Tiene algo para el dolor de estómago?	*Do you have something for a stomachache?*
Farmacéutico	¿Qué le ocurre?	*What's wrong with you?*
Thomas	No lo sé. Comí algo anoche, y no me siento muy bien.	*I don't know. I ate something last night, and now I don't feel very well.*
Farmacéutico	¿Tiene diarrea o náuseas? ¿O es un dolor agudo?	*Do you have diarrhea or are you nauseous? Or is it a sharp pain?*
Thomas	Es más bien un malestar general.	*I just don't feel well in general.*
Farmacéutico	¿Consultó a un médico?	*Did you see a doctor?*
Thomas	Todavía no. ¿Necesito una receta?	*Not yet. Do I need a prescription?*
Farmacéutico	Para estas pastillas no, pero si usted se siente mal mañana, le aconsejo que vea a un médico.	*Not for these pills, but if you still feel sick tomorrow, I advise you to go to a doctor.*
Thomas	Primero voy a ver si estas pastillas me ayudan.	*First I'll see if these pills help me.*
Farmacéutico	Tome dos cada cuatro horas. Espero que se mejore.	*Take two every four hours. I hope you feel better.*

Going to the Doctor
Story

Médica	¿Hace cuánto tiempo que se siente mal?	*How long has he been feeling ill?*
Karen	Desde hace dos días.	*For two days.*
Médica	¿Te duele la cabeza? ¿Sientes débil las piernas? ¿Sientes vértigo?	*Does your head hurt? Do you feel weak in the legs? Are you dizzy?*
Johnny	Sí, es un poco de todo. No sé qué me ocurre.	*Yes, it's a little of everything. I don't know what's wrong with me.*

continued...

LEARN TO SPEAK SPANISH

Going to the Doctor
Story: continued

Médica	Es posible que sea el efecto de la altitud. Es frecuente cuando uno no está acostumbrado.	*It's possible that it's the effect of the altitude. It's common when one isn't used to it.*
Karen	¿Y qué me recomienda usted?	*And what do you recommend that I do?*
Médica	Debe tener cuidado con las comidas y las bebidas.	*You should be careful about food and drink.*
Médica	Por ejemplo, él debe evitar las comidas pesadas con mucha grasa.	*For example, he should avoid heavy greasy foods.*
Johnny	¿Necesito tomar alguna medicina especial?	*Do I need to take any special medicine?*
Médica	No, no es preciso. Se te pasará pronto.	*No, it isn't necessary. It will go away soon.*
Médica	Que él trate de descansar, y sobre todo, usted no se preocupe.	*He should try to rest, and above all, don't worry.*

Action

Médico	¿Hace cuánto tiempo que se siente mal?	*How long have you been feeling ill?*
Thomas	Desde hace dos días.	*For two days.*
Médico	¿Le duele la cabeza? ¿Siente débil las piernas? ¿Siente vértigo?	*Does your head hurt? Do you feel weak in the legs? Are you dizzy?*
Thomas	Sí, es un poco de todo. No sé qué me ocurre.	*Yes, it's a little of everything. I don't know what's wrong with me.*
Médico	Es posible que sea el efecto de la altitud. Es frecuente cuando uno no está acostumbrado.	*It's possible that it's the effect of the altitude. It's common when one isn't used to it.*
Thomas	¿Y qué me recomienda usted?	*And what do you recommend that I do?*
Médico	Debe tener cuidado con la comida y las bebidas.	*You should be careful about food and drink.*

continued...

Going to the Doctor
Action: continued

Médico	Por ejemplo, evite las comidas pesadas con mucha grasa y también las bebidas alcohólicas.	*For example, avoid heavy greasy foods and also alcoholic beverages.*
Médico	Trate de descansar, y sobre todo, no se preocupe. Se le pasará pronto.	*Try to rest, and above all, don't worry. It will go away soon.*
Thomas	¿Necesito tomar alguna medicina especial?	*Do I need to take any special medicine?*
Médico	No, no es preciso.	*No, it isn't necessary.*

Going to the Dry Cleaner
Story

Empleada	Entonces, cuatro camisas, dos pantalones, un traje, seis pares de calcetines, cuatro calzoncillos y tres camisetas.	*Let's see, four shirts, two pairs of pants, a suit, six pairs of socks, four pairs of underwear, and three undershirts.*
Empleada	¿Para cuándo los quiere?	*When do you want them?*
Mario	Lo más pronto posible.	*As soon as possible.*
Mario	También necesito que me ponga un botón en la camisa azul.	*I also need you to sew a button on the blue shirt.*
Mario	El ruedo del pantalón negro está suelto. ¿Puede arreglarmelo?	*The hem of the black pants is loose. Can you fix it?*
Empleada	¡Cómo no, señor!	*Of course, sir.*
Empleada	¿Quiere que le ponga almidón en las camisas y que le planche todo?	*Do you want me to put starch in the shirts and iron everything?*
Mario	Sí, está bien. Pero no ponga demasiado almidón en las camisas.	*Yes, fine. But don't put too much starch in the shirts.*
Empleada	Estará todo listo mañana por la tarde.	*Everything will be ready tomorrow afternoon.*
Mario	¿No puede ser por la mañana?	*Can't it be in the morning?*
Empleada	No puede ser antes porque tenemos muchos encargos acumulados.	*It can't be sooner than that because we have a lot of orders ahead of yours.*
Mario	De acuerdo. Hasta mañana.	*O.K. See you tomorrow.*

Going to the Dry Cleaner
Action

Empleada	Entonces, cuatro camisas, dos pantalones, un traje, seis pares de calcetines, cuatro calzoncillos y tres camisetas.	*Let's see, four shirts, two pairs of pants, a suit, six pairs of socks, four pairs of underwear, and three undershirts.*
Empleada	¿Para cuándo los quiere?	*When do you want them?*
Thomas	Lo más pronto posible. También necesito que me ponga un botón en la camisa azul.	*As soon as possible. I also need you to sew a button on the blue shirt.*
Thomas	El ruedo del pantalón negro está suelto. ¿Puede arreglármelo?	*The hem of the black pants is loose. Can you fix it?*
Empleada	¡Cómo no, señor! ¿Quiere que le ponga almidón en las camisas y que le planche todo?	*Of course, sir. Do you want me to put starch in the shirts and iron everything?*
Thomas	Sí, está bien. Pero no ponga demasiado almidón en las camisas.	*Yes, fine. But don't put too much starch in the shirts.*
Empleada	Estará todo listo mañana por la tarde.	*Everything will be ready tomorrow afternoon.*
Thomas	¿No puede ser en la mañana?	*Can't it be in the morning?*
Empleada	No puede ser antes porque tenemos muchos encargos acumulados.	*It can't be sooner than that because we have a lot of orders ahead of yours.*
Thomas	De acuerdo. Hasta mañana.	*O.K. See you tomorrow.*

Finding an Apartment
Story

Mario	Estoy buscando una casa o un apartamento para cuatro personas. Somos un matrimonio y dos hijos.	*I'm looking for a house or an apartment for four persons. We're a married couple and two children.*
Agente	¿Desea una casa dentro de la ciudad o en las afueras?	*Do you want a house in the city or in the suburbs?*
Agente	Fuera de la ciudad tiene usted la ventaja del precio y del espacio.	*Outside the city you have the advantage of better prices and more space.*

continued...

Finding an Apartment
Story: continued

Mario	No, a mi esposa no le gusta vivir en el campo porque le lleva mucho tiempo llegar al trabajo.	*No, my wife doesn't like to live in the country because it takes her too long to get to work.*
Agente	Podemos ofrecerle una casa cerca del centro con seis dormitorios, cocina, comedor, dos cuartos de baño y una sala de estar.	*We can offer you a house near the downtown area with six bedrooms, kitchen and dining room, two bathrooms, and a living room.*
Agente	También tiene un garaje de dos plazas y un patio. Pero no está amueblada.	*It also has a two car garage and a patio. But it isn't furnished.*
Mario	No, es que vamos a estar aquí sólo un año. Necesitamos una vivienda amueblada.	*No, we're only going to be here for a year. We need a place that's furnished.*

Action

Thomas	Estoy buscando una casa o un apartamento para cuatro personas. Somos un matrimonio y dos hijos.	*I'm looking for a house or an apartment for four persons. We're a married couple and two children.*
Agente	¿Desea una casa dentro de la ciudad o en las afueras?	*Do you want a house in the city or in the suburbs?*
Agente	Fuera de la ciudad tiene usted la ventaja del precio y del espacio.	*Outside the city you have the advantage of better prices and more space.*
Thomas	No, porque me lleva mucho tiempo llegar al trabajo. Y a mi esposa no le gusta vivir en el campo.	*No, because it would take me too long to get to work. And my wife doesn't like to live in the country.*
Agente	Podemos ofrecerle una casa cerca del centro con seis dormitorios, cocina y comedor, dos cuartos de baño y una sala de estar.	*We can offer you a house near the downtown area with six bedrooms, kitchen and dining room, two bathrooms, and a living room.*

continued…

Finding an Apartment
Action: continued

Agente	También tiene un garaje de dos plazas y un patio. Pero no está amueblada.	*It also has a two car garage and a patio. But it isn't furnished.*
Thomas	No, es que vamos a estar aquí sólo un año. Necesitamos una vivienda amueblada.	*No, we're only going to be here for a year. We need a place that's furnished.*

Talking About Going Shopping
Story

Karen	Necesito comprar carne, pescado, verduras, huevos, leche y fruta.	*I need to buy meat, fish, vegetables, eggs, milk and fruit.*
Silvia	Bueno, mira, en este mercado puedes compara lo que quieras.	*Fine, look, in this market you can buy whatever you want.*
Silvia	En esta parte tienes la carne de cerdo y de res. El pescado está un poco más lejos, a la derecha.	*In this part, you can have the pork and beef. The fish is a little further ahead, on the right.*
Silvia	Y a continuación, podemos comprar la fruta y las verduras.	*And farther on, we can buy fruit and vegetables.*
Karen	¿Es más barato comprar aquí o en el supermercado?	*Is it cheaper to shop here or at the supermarket?*
Silvia	Normalmente, aquí es más barato, y los productos son más frescos, sobre todo las verduras.	*Normally it's cheaper here, and the products are fresher, especially the vegetables.*
Karen	También necesito comprar harina.	*I also need to buy flour.*
Silvia	La harina tienes que comprarla en el supermercado. Aquí no la tienen.	*You have to buy flour at the supermarket. They don't have it here.*
Karen	Bueno, vamos a empezar con las verduras.	*O.K. Let's start with the vegetables.*

Talking About Going Shopping
Action

Elena	Necesito comprar carne, pescado, verduras, huevos, leche y fruta.	*I need to buy meat, fish, vegetables, eggs, milk and fruit.*
Silvia	Bueno, mira, en este mercado puedes comprar lo que quieras.	*Fine, look, in this market you can buy whatever you want.*
Silvia	En esta parte tienes la carne de cerdo y de res. El pescado está un poco más lejos, a la derecha.	*In this part, you can have the pork and beef. The fish is a little further ahead, on the right.*
Silvia	Y a continuación, podemos comprar la fruta y las verduras.	*And farther on, we can buy fruit and vegetables.*
Elena	¿Es más barato comprar aquí o en el supermercado?	*Is it cheaper to shop here or at the supermarket?*
Silvia	Normalmente, aquí es más barato, y los productos son más frescos, sobre todo las verduras.	*Normally it's cheaper here, and the products are fresher, especially the vegetables.*
Elena	También necesito comprar harina.	*I also need to buy flour.*
Silvia	La harina tienes que comprarla en el supermercado. Aquí no la tienen.	*You have to buy flour at the supermarket. They don't have it here.*
Elena	Bueno, vamos a empezar por la carnicería.	*O.K. Let's start at the meat counter.*

Going to the Market
Story

Mario	Deme dos kilos de chuletas de cerdo, uno de ternera y uno de salchichas.	*Give me two kilos of pork chops, one of veal, and one of sausages.*
Carnicero	¿Algo más?	*Anything else?*
Mario	No, gracias. ¿Puede envolverlo todo y meterlo en una bolsa de plástico?	*No, thanks. Can you wrap it all up and put it in a plastic bag?*
Carnicero	¡Cómo no! Aquí tiene.	*Of course. Here you are.*
Mario	Quiero medio kilo de limones, cuatro de naranjas, dos de bananas y una sandia.	*I want half a kilo of lemons, four of oranges, two of bananas and a watermelon.*

continued…

Going to the Market
Story: continued

Frutera	La sandia pesa más de cinco kilos.	*The watermelon weighs over five kilos.*
Frutera	¿Quiere usted una más pequeña? .	*Do you want a smaller one?*
Mario	No, ésa está bien.	*No, that one is fine.*
Johnny	Si seguimos comprando tanto, vamos a necesitar una empleada para ayudarte con las compras.	*If we keep buying so much, we're going to need a maid to help us do the shopping.*

Action

Elena	Deme dos kilos de chuletas de cerdo, uno de ternera y uno de salchichas.	*Give me two kilos of pork chops, one of veal, and one of sausages.*
Carnicero	¿Algo más?	*Anything else?*
Elena	No, gracias. ¿Puede envolverlo todo y meterlo en una bolsa de plástico?	*No, thanks. Can you wrap it all up and put it in a plastic bag?*
Carnicero	¡Cómo no! Aquí tiene.	*Of course. Here you are.*
Elena	Quiero medio kilo de limones, cuatro de naranjas, dos de bananas y una sandía.	*I want half a kilo of lemons, four of oranges, two of bananas and a watermelon.*
Frutero	La sandía pesa más de cinco kilos. ¿Quiere usted una más pequeña?	*The watermelon weighs over five kilos. Do you want a smaller one?*
Elena	No, ésa está bien.	*No, that one is fine.*
Silvia	Si sigues comprando tanto, vas a necesitar a una empleada para ayudarte con las compras.	*If you keep buying so much, you're going to need a maid to help you do the shopping*

Talking to the Maid
Story

Karen	Lupe, no te olvides de cambiar las sábanas hoy antes de hacer las camas.	*Lupe, don't forget to change the sheets today before you make the beds.*
Lupe	¿Paso primero la aspiradora en la sala?	*Should I run the vacuum cleaner in the living room first?*
Karen	No, arregla primero los dormitorios y barre después el pasillo. Deja la sala para el final.	*No, first straighten up the edrooms and then sweep the hallway. Leave the living room for last.*
Lupe	¿Cuándo quiere que lave la ropa?	*When do you want me to wash the clothes?*
Karen	La lavadora no funciona. Voy a llamar esta tarde a un técnico para que arregle el aparato.	*The washing machine isn't working. I'm going to call this afternoon a repairman to come and fix the machine.*
Karen	Lleva la ropa a la lavandería cuando vayas a hacer las compras.	*Take the clothes to the laundry when you go to do the shopping.*
Lupe	¿Quiere que limpie las ventanas también?	*Do you want me to wash the windows too?*
Karen	Bueno, si tienes tiempo hoy, limpia las ventanas y quita el polvo a los muebles.	*Sure, if you have time today, wash the windows and dust the furniture.*
Lupe	A ver cuánto tardo en el mercado.	*I'll see how long it takes me at the market.*

Action

Elena	Lupe, no te olvides de cambiar las sábanas hoy antes de hacer las camas.	*Lupe, don't forget to change the sheets today before you make the beds.*
Lupe	¿Paso primero la aspiradora en la sala?	*Should I run the vacuum cleaner in the living room first?*
Elena	No, arregla primero los dormitorios y barre después el pasillo. Deja la sala para el final.	*No, first straighten up the bedrooms and then sweep the hallway. Leave the living room for last.*

continued...

Talking to the Maid
Action: continued

Lupe	¿Cuándo quiere que lave la ropa?	*When do you want me to wash the clothes?*
Elena	La lavadora no funciona. Lleva la ropa a la lavandería cuando vayas a hacer las compras.	*The washing machine isn't working. Take the clothes to the laundry when you go to do the shopping.*
Elena	Voy a llamar esta tarde a un técnico para que arregle el aparato.	*I'm going to call this afternoon a repairman to come and fix the machine.*
Lupe	¿Quiere que limpie las ventanas también?	*Do you want me to wash the windows too?*
Elena	Bueno, si tienes tiempo hoy, limpia las ventanas y quita el polvo a los muebles.	*Sure, if you have time today, wash the windows and dust the furniture.*
Lupe	A ver cuánto tardo en el mercado.	*I'll see how long it takes me at the market.*

Talking About Buying Clothing
Story

Mario	¿Encontraste el vestido que buscabas?	*Did you find the dress that you were looking for?*
Karen	No. Había uno negro que me gustaba mucho pero la talla era demasiado grande para mí.	*No, there was a black one that I liked a lot but the size was too large for me.*
Mario	¿No tenían tallas más pequeñas?	*Didn't they have smaller sizes?*
Karen	Sí, pero no en negro. Había uno amarillo horroroso.	*Yes, but not in black. There was a yellow one that was horrible.*
Karen	Encontré una bluse muy linda que hace juego con mi falda gris.	*I found a very pretty blouse that matches my gray skirt.*
Karen	¿Y tú, compraste los zapatos?	*And you, did you buy some shoes?*
Mario	Sí. Encontré unos zapatos de cuero a muy buen precio.	*Yes. I found some leather shoes at a very good price.*

continued...

Talking About Buying Clothing
Story: continued

Mario	También compré un traje nuevo.	*I also bought a new suit.*
Karen	¿Otro traje? ¡Tienes ya tantos!	*Another suit? You already have so many!*
Mario	Sólo tengo tres y todos viejos.	*I only have three and they're all old.*
Mario	Lo que necesito ahora son camisas.	*What I need now are shirts.*
Karen	Yo iré contigo a comprarlas.	*I'll go with you to buy them.*
Mario	Siempre tienes buen gusto, ¿sabes?	*You always have the best of taste, you know.*
Mario	De paso me aconsejas con los pantalones.	*You can give me some advice about the pants then, while you're at it.*

Action

Thomas	¿Encontraste el vestido que buscabas?	*Did you find the dress that you were looking for?*
Elena	No. Había uno negro que me gustaba mucho pero la talla era demasiado grande para mí.	*No, there was a black one that I liked a lot but the size was too large for me.*
Thomas	¿No tenían tallas más pequeñas?	*Didn't they have smaller sizes?*
Elena	Sí, pero no en negro. Había uno amarillo horroroso.	*Yes, but not in black. There was a yellow one that was horrible.*
Elena	Encontré una blusa muy linda que hace juego con mi falda gris. ¿Y tú, compraste los zapatos?	*I found a very pretty blouse that matches my gray skirt. And you, did you buy some shoes?*
Thomas	Sí. Encontré unos zapatos de cuero a muy buen precio. También compré un traje nuevo.	*Yes. I found some leather shoes at a very good price. I also bought a new suit.*
Elena	¿Otro traje? ¡Tienes ya tantos!	*Another suit? You already have so many!*
Thomas	Sólo tengo tres y todos viejos. Lo que necesito ahora son camisas.	*I only have three and they're all old. What I need now are shirts.*

continued...

Talking About Buying Clothing
Action: continued

Elena	Yo iré contigo a comprarlas. No siempre tienes buen gusto, ¿sabes?	*I'll go with you to buy them. You don't always have the best of taste, you know.*
Thomas	De paso me aconsejas con los pantalones.	*You can give me some advice about the pants, then, while you're at it.*

At the Gas Station
Story

Mario	Lléneme el tanque con super, por favor.	*Fill the tank with super, please.*
Empleado	Sí señor.	*Yes, sir.*
Empleado	Me parece que tiene una llanta desinflada. ¿Quiere que le ponga aire?	*I think you have a flat tire. Do you want me to put some air in it?*
Mario	Ah, sí, por favor. ¿Puede revisarme también el aceite y el agua?	*Oh, yes, please. Can you also check the oil and the water for me?*
Empleado	Ahora mismo. Todo está bien, pero le puse un poco de aceite.	*Right away. Everything's fine, but I put in a little oil.*
Mario	Bien. ¿Puedo pagar con tarjeta de crédito?	*Good. Can I pay with a credit card?*
Empleado	No señor. Tiene usted que pagar en efectivo. No aceptamos tarjetas.	*No, sir. You have to pay cash. We don't take credit cards.*
Mario	No sé si va a alcanzarme.	*I don't know if I have enough.*
Mario	¿Cuánto es?	*How much it is?*
Empleado	Treinta pesos.	*Thirty pesos.*
Mario	Ah, pues sí, mire. Tengo justo esa cantidad. Aquí tiene.	*Oh, yes, look. I have just that amount. Here you are.*
Empleado	Espere a que le limpie el parabrisas.	*Wait until I clean your windshield.*

At the Gas Station
Action

Elena	Lléneme el tanque con super, por favor.	*Fill the tank with super, please.*
Empleado	Sí, señora. Me parece que tiene una llanta desinflada. ¿Quiere que le ponga aire?	*Yes, ma'am. I think you have a flat tire. Do you want me to put some air in it?*
Elena	Ah, sí, por favor. ¿Puede revisarme también el aceite y el agua?	*Oh, yes, please. Can you also check the oil and the water for me?*
Empleado	Ahora mismo. Todo está bien, pero le puse un poco de aceite.	*Right away. Everything's fine, but I put in a little oil.*
Elena	Bien. ¿Puedo pagar con tarjeta de crédito?	*Good. Can I pay with a credit card?*
Empleado	No señora. Tiene usted que pagar en efectivo. No aceptamos tarjetas.	*No, ma'am. You have to pay cash. We don't take credit cards.*
Elena	No sé si va a alcanzarme. ¿Cuánto es?	*I don't know if I have enough. How much it is?*
Empleado	Treinta pesos.	*Thirty pesos.*
Elena	Ah, pues sí, mire. Tengo justo esa cantidad. Aquí tiene.	*Oh, yes, look. I have just that amount. Here you are.*
Empleado	Espere a que le limpie el parabrisas.	*Wait until I clean your windshield.*

Talking About Family
Story

Karen	Hemos recibido una carta de tus padres hoy. Dicen que estuvieron en Florida con tu hermano.	*We got a letter from your parents today. They said they were in Florida with your brother.*
Mario	¿Y qué más?	*And what else?*
Karen	Están pensando en venir de vacaciones para Navidad, pero tu mamá no sabe si tendrá muchos días libres.	*They're thinking about coming for a vacation at Christmas, but your mom doesn't know if she'll have many days free.*

continued...

Talking About Family
Story: continued

Mario	¡Qué raro! Ella ya no trabaja.	*How strange! She doesn't work any more.*
Karen	No, pero tu cuñada quiere pasar unos días con ellos en esas fechas. Sabes que les gusta ver a sus nietos.	*No, but your sister in-law wants to spend a few days with them then. You know they like to see their grandkids.*
Mario	¡Pues aquí tienen dos nietos también!	*Well they have two grandchildren here too!*
Karen	No es para tomarlo a mal.	*Don't take it the wrong way.*
Karen	Pueden venir en Semana Santa. Hace mejor tiempo y también es el cumpleaños del pequeño.	*They can come here for Easter week. The weather's better, and it's also the baby's birthday.*
Mario	Como tú quieras.	*Have it your way.*

Action

Elena	Hemos recibido carta de tus padres hoy. Dicen que estuvieron en Florida con tu hermano.	*We got a letter from your parents today. They said they were in Florida with your brother.*
Thomas	¿Y qué más?	*And what else?*
Elena	Están pensando en venir de vacaciones para Navidad, pero tu mamá no sabe si tendrá muchos días libres.	*They're thinking about coming for a vacation at Christmas, but your mom doesn't know if she'll have many days free.*
Thomas	¡Qué raro! Ella ya no trabaja.	*How strange! She doesn't work any more.*
Elena	No, pero tu cuñada quiere pasar unos días con ellos en esas fechas. Sabes que les gusta ver a sus nietos.	*No, but your sister in law wants to spend a few days with them then. You know how much they like to see their grandchildren.*
Thomas	¡Pues aquí tienen dos nietos también!	*Well they have two grandchildren here too!*

continued...

Everyday Life

Talking About Family
Action: continued

Elena	No es para tomarlo a mal. Pueden venir en Semana Santa.	*Don't take it the wrong way. They can come here for Easter week.*
Elena	Hace mejor tiempo y también es el cumpleaños del pequeño.	*The weather's better, and it's also the baby's birthday.*
Thomas	Como tú quieras.	*Have it your way.*

Going to the Beauty Salon
Story

Susy	Quería cortarme el pelo, pero no mucho. Sólo las puntas. El flequillo déjelo como está.	*I wanted to cut my hair, but not very much. Just the ends. Leave the bangs the way they are.*
Peluquera	¿Quiere lavarse el pelo antes?	*Do you want a shampoo first?*
Susy	Sí, pero tengo el pelo muy seco. ¿Puede ponerme un buen acondicionador?	*Yes, but my hair's very dry. Can you put a good conditioner on it?*
Peluquera	¡Cómo no!	*Of course!*
Peluquera	¿No piensa usted hacerse una permanente? Le quedaría muy bien.	*Of course! You're not thinking about getting a permanent? It would look good on you.*
Susy	Sí, ya lo he pensado	*Yes, I've thought about it.*
Susy	Lo que pasa es que a mi no me gustan los rizos.	*The problem is that I don't like curls.*
Peluquera	No, es que le daría un poco más de volúmen.	*No, it would just give you a little more body.*
Susy	Eso me vendría bien a mí porque no quiero parecer calva.	*That's what I need, because I don't want to look bald.*

Action

Elena	Quería cortarme el pelo, pero no mucho. Sólo las puntas. El flequillo déjelo como está.	*I wanted to cut my hair, but not very much. Just the ends. Leave the bangs the way they are.*
Peluquera	¿Quiere lavarse el pelo antes?	*Do you want a shampoo first?*

continued…

49

Going to the Beauty Salon
Action: continued

Elena	Sí, pero tengo el pelo muy seco. ¿Puede ponerme un buen acondicionador?	*Yes, but my hair's very dry. Can you put a good conditioner on it?*
Peluquera	¡Cómo no! ¿No piensa usted hacerse una permanente? Le quedaría muy bien.	*Of course! You're not thinking about getting a permanent? It would look good on you.*
Elena	Sí, ya lo he pensado. Lo que pasa es que a mi marido no le gustan los rizos.	*Yes, I've thought about it. The problem is that my husband doesn't like curls.*
Peluquera	No, es que le daría un poco más de volumen.	*No, it would just give you a little more body.*
Elena	Eso le vendría bien a mi marido porque se está quedando casi calvo.	*That's what my husband needs, because he's practically going bald.*
Peluquera	El problema con los hombres es que no se cuidan mucho.	*The problem with men is that they don't take good care of themselves.*

Grammar Topics
NOUNS
Gender of Nouns

In Spanish, all nouns are either masculine or feminine in gender. This is merely a grammatical concept; it does not mean that Spanish speakers perceive things as having male or female attributes. Nouns that refer to male people or animals, and most nouns that end in -*o* are masculine in gender. (One common exception is l*a mano*, "the hand"). Most nouns that refer to female people or animals, and most nouns that end in -*a, -ción, -dad* or -*tad* are feminine in gender. (Some exceptions are *el día, el problema, el drama,* and *el programa*). Nouns that have other endings, or nouns that are exceptions to the rules, must be memorized: *el billete, el dólar, el valor,* etc.

Plural of Nouns

Spanish nouns that end in a vowel form plurals by adding the letter -*s*. Nouns that end in a consonant add -*es*. Nouns that end in the consonant -*z* change the -*z* to -*c* before adding -*es: el lápiz* ("pencil"), pl. *los lápices*. Nouns that have the last syllable accented in the singular form will lose the accent mark when the noun is plural: *la conversación, las conversaciones; la razón* ("reason"), *las razones,* etc.

As well, when the noun is plural the definite and indefinite articles must be used in the plural form: *un hombre>unos hombres; la conversación>las conversaciones. Unos* and *unas* mean some, several or a few.

In Spanish, the masculine plural form of a noun is used when referring to a group made up of males and females: *los amigos* (includes both male and female friends).

Definite and Indefinite Articles

In English, the definite article is "the," and the indefinite article is "a," or "an". In Spanish, the articles have four forms, and they must agree with the noun in number (singular or plural) and gender (masculine or feminine). See the following:

	MASCULINE	FEMININE
Definite Articles	el	la (singular)
	los	las (plural)

Indefinite Articles   **un** ....**una** **(singular)**
                               unos ....**unas** **(plural)**

Examples: *el aeropuerto, los billetes, la empleada, las oficinas, un hombre, unos dólares, una señora, unas conversaciones.*

Contractions *Del* and *Al*

In Spanish, there are only two contractions, *del* and *al*, and they are obligatory. Whenever you have the definite article el immediately following the preposition *de*, you must make the contraction *del*. Whenever you have the definite article *el* immediately following the preposition *a*, you must make the contraction *al*.

Es el dinero del señor González. (de + el)
Vamos al hotel. (a + el)

Note: *De* and *a* do not contract with any of the other articles.

Es el dinero de la señor García.
Es el dinero de los pasajeros.
Vamos a la oficina.
Vamos a las reuniones.

In Spanish, the word *a* immediately precedes the direct object of a sentence when the direct object refers to a specific person or persons. This personal *a*, which has no equivalent in English, forms contractions in the same manner as the preposition *a*.

Thomas llama a la secretaria.
Thomas llama al secretario.
Voy a ver a la señor Garcia.
Voy a ver al señor Garcia.

PRONOUNS
Subject Pronouns

The subject pronoun which indicates who is doing the action generally precedes the verb. The forms are:

SINGULAR		PLURAL	
I	**yo**	we	**nosotros, nosotras**
you (informal)	**tú**	you (informal)	**vosotros, vosotras**
you (formal)	**usted**	you (formal)	**ustedes**
it, he	**él**	they	**ellos**
it, she	**ella**	they	**ellas**

Nosotros and *vosotros* have feminine forms (*nosotras, vosotras*) when referring to a group made up entirely of women. If the group contains both males and females, the masculine form is used. Similarly, *ellos* can refer to a group made up of both men and women, while *ellas* refers to a group made up entirely of females.

Use of Subject Pronouns

Because most verb endings in Spanish tell who is doing the action, it is not necessary to use the subject pronouns in most cases: *Trabajo en esta compañia* (the verb ending *-o* indicates that the subject of the sentence is "I"). Only when there is a chance of confusion, or if the speaker wants to emphasize who is doing the action, is the subject pronoun used: *Ella es española, pero él es norteamericano* (the verb *es* can have as a subject "he" and "she"); *Yo quiero comer ahora* (the *yo* is used only for emphasis, but is not necessary).

In English, the subject "it" is always mentioned: "it is interesting," "here it is," "where is it?," etc. In Spanish, however, the subject pronoun "it" is rarely, if ever, expressed. The verb stands alone, and the subject "it" is understood: *Es interesante, aquí está, ¿dónde está? etc.*

Formal and Informal "You"

Spanish has two forms of "you," the formal (*usted* [Ud.] *ustedes* [Uds.]) and the informal (*tú, vosotros*). There are no hard and fast rules for when to use one form or the other but, in general, if you know the person well enough to call him or her by his or her first name, use *tú*. If you address the person by Mr., Miss, or Mrs. with a last name, use *usted* (commonly abbreviated as *Ud.*) If you are unsure about which form to use, it is better to start off with *usted*. The native speaker can suggest that you use *tú* if it is more appropriate.

In Spain, a distinction is made between the plural forms *ustedes* (formal) and *vosotros/vosotras* (informal). In Spanish America, however, *ustedes* is used for both formal and informal situations. Use the plural whenever you are directly addressing more than one person.

Direct Object Pronouns

The direct object of a sentence answers the question "what?" or "whom?": "What do you want to see?" ("The city"); "Whom do you see on the balcony?" ("My wife"). To replace the direct object noun with a pronoun, you must choose the correct direct object pronoun, the one that reflects the number and gender of the noun it replaces:

me . . . . .me	**nos** . . . . .us
te . . . . .you (informal)	**os** . . . . .you all (informal)
lo, la . . . . . . .you (formal)	**los, las** . . . . . . .you (formal)
lo, la . . . . . . .him, her, it	**los, las** . . . . . . .them

Notice that the direct object pronouns, like the indirect object pronouns, immediately precede the conjugated verb: (*¿A mí?*) *Sí, ellos me conocen.* (*¿A Elena?*) *Yo no la conozco.* (*¿El dinero?*) *Lo tengo aquí.* (*¿Las maletas?*) *No las veo.*

The pronoun can instead be attached to an infinitive: *Lo voy a ver* or *Voy a verlo. Te quiero ayudar* or *Quiero ayudarte.*

Indirect Object Pronouns

The indirect object of a sentence usually answers the question "to whom?" or "for whom?": *Roberto me da un regalo* ("Roberto gives a present to me"); *Yo te compro este libro* ("I'll buy this book for you). To replace the indirect object noun with a pronoun, you must choose the correct form that corresponds to the noun:

me . . . . .to me	**nos** . . . . .to us
te . . . . .to you (informal)	**os** . . . . .to you all (informal)
le . . . . .to you (formal)	**les** . . . . .to you all (formal)
le . . . . .to him, to her	**les** . . . . .to them

Sometimes native speakers will use *le* or *les* as both the direct and indirect object pronoun when they are referring to a male person. If you are not sure which form to use (*le* or *lo*) when talking about a man, you can almost always use *le*.

Placement of Object Pronouns

Both direct and indirect object pronouns immediately precede a conjugated verb:
Thomas le pide el número; Ahora mismo le doy el regalo; Roberto me recibe y me hace pasar; Yo te indico dónde está la oficina; No lo conocemos.

These pronoun forms can also be attached to an infinitive: *¿Puede decirme dónde están los servicios?; Podemos hacerle un precio especial; ¿Vas a llamarme?* They can also be attached to gerunds: *Estoy comprándoles los libros; Estamos buscándolo.*

With an affirmative command, the pronoun is also attached to the end of the verb: *(¿Las maletas?) Póngalas aquí; Déjelo; Tráigame una cerveza.*

With a negative command, the pronoun precedes the verb: *No las ponga allí; No me diga.*

Sequence of Object Pronouns

When both a direct and indirect object pronoun appear in a sentence, the indirect object pronoun will precede the direct object pronoun: *Me lo dice; Te la mando ahora.* When both the direct and indirect object pronouns are in the third person, the indirect object pronoun must be replaced by *se*:

indirect object + direct object
le, les + lo/la/los/las

¿Le das los libros a Silvia?	Are you giving the books to Silvia?
Sí, se los doy.	Yes, I'm giving them to her.
¿Les compras los juguetes?	Are you buying the toys for them?
Sí, se los compro.	Yes, I'm buying them for them.
¿Me trae un café?	Will you bring me a coffee?
Sí, se lo traigo ahora.	Yes, I'll bring it to you [formal] now.

Note that when object pronouns are attached to affirmative commands, gerunds, or infinitives, you may need to add an accent mark to preserve the stress of the word: *Búscalo; Estoy buscándolo; Tráigamelo; Voy a traérselo; but Voy a traerlo.*

LEARN TO SPEAK SPANISH

Some Uses of *Se*

1. As the impersonal subject "you," "one," "people": *Se come bien en este restaurante.* ("One eats well in this restaurant."); *¿Cómo se dice "today" en español?* ("How does one say 'today' in Spanish?"); *Nunca se sabe* ("One never knows"). Notice that in this construction, the verb is always in the third person singular.

2. In passive constructions: *Aquí se habla español* ("Spanish is spoken here"); *Se venden libros* ("Books are sold"). Notice that in these constructions the verb may be in the third person singular or plural, depending on whether the thing you're referring to (the grammatical subject) is singular or plural.

3. With a reflexive verb to indicate that the subject and object of the action are the same person: *Roberto se viste.* ("Roberto is getting dressed.")

4. To express mutual or reciprocal actions, generally expressed in English as "each other": *Elena y Thomas se besan.* ("Elena and Thomas are kissing each other.")

Some Uses of *Lo*

The word *lo* can be a direct object pronoun; "him," "it," "you" but it can also function as a neuter article to describe an abstract idea. In English, this structure is usually expressed by "the...thing." *Lo más importante es que ustedes lleguen a tiempo* ("The most important thing is that you all arrive on time"). *Lo malo es que Thomas no puede encontrar una casa amueblada*("The bad thing is that Thomas can't find a furnished house").

Lo can also refer to a whole situation: *déjelo* ("forget the whole thing"). *No lo comprendo* ("I don't understand anything").

Possessive Pronouns

A possessive pronoun is used to replace a noun phrase that starts with a possessive adjective.

Examples:

I like <u>your dress.</u> . . . . I like <u>yours</u>.

She likes <u>their house</u>. . . . . She likes <u>theirs.</u>

The Spanish possessive pronouns are used with the definite articles and agree in number and gender with the object possessed, not with the speaker.

The possessive pronouns in Spanish are:

SINGULAR	PLURAL
el mío . . . .**la mía**	**los míos** . . . .**las mías**
el tuyo . . . .**la tuya**	**los tuyos** . . . .**las tuyas**
el suyo . . . .**la suya**	**los suyos** . . . .**las suyas**
el nuestro . . . . . .**la nuestra**	**los nuestros** . . . .**las nuestras**
el vuestro . . . . . .**la vuestra**	**los vuestros** . . . .**las vuestras**
el suyo . . . .**la suya**	**los suyos** . . . .**las suyas**

To select the right possessive pronoun, one needs to determine the gender and number of the object possessed and the person to whom it belongs.

Examples:
*Me gusta **tu reloj**. . . . . .I like your watch.
Me gusta **el tuyo**. . . . . .I like yours.

In this case, *el tuyo* replaces *tu reloj* because the object (*reloj*) is masculine singular and belongs to "*tú*", the second person singular.

***Nuestra casa** está a la venta. . . . . .Our house is for sale.
La nuestra está a la venta. . . . . .Ours is for sale.

In this case, *la nuestra* replaces nuestra casa because the object (*casa*) is feminine singular and belongs to "*nosotros*", the first person plural.

ADJECTIVES & ADVERBS
Agreement of Adjectives

Adjectives of nationality and adjectives that end in -*o* have four forms in Spanish to reflect gender (masculine, feminine) and number (singular, plural). The adjective must agree in gender and number with the noun it describes: *el hombre mexicano, la mujer mexicana, los hombres mexicanos, las mujeres mexicanas, un hotel bueno, una cerveza buena, unos hoteles buenos, unas cervezas buenas,* etc.

Adjectives that end in -*e* or in a consonant have only two forms; singular and plural. These adjectives do not normally reflect gender: *un hombre interesante, una mujer interesante, unos hombres interesantes, unas mujeres interesantes, un precio especial, una comida especial, unos precios especiales, unas comidas especiales.*

Placement of Adjectives

Adjectives that describe the qualities of a noun (what something or someone is like) generally follow the noun in Spanish: *un precio especial, un hotel bueno, una mujer inteligente,* etc. Adjectives of quantity and demonstrative adjectives precede the noun: *cinco habitaciones, muchos taxis, pocas personas, otro día, este día, esta noche.*

Occasionally, you will notice that native speakers change some of these rules. For example, you may sometimes hear a native speaker place a descriptive adjective in front of the noun: *un nuevo chofer, un buen día, unos excelentes hoteles.* These changes are for stylistic purposes and only slightly alter the meaning, placing more emphasis on the adjective than usual. An exception to this is *grande.* Before a noun, *grande* becomes *gran,* and means "important" or "great."

Possessive Adjectives

The most common way to express possession in Spanish is with what are referred to as the unstressed possessive adjectives:

SINGULAR	PLURAL
mi, mis- my	**nuestro/a/os/as-** our
tu, tus- your, informal	**uestro/a/os/as-** your, informal [Spain]
su, sus- your, formal	**su, sus-** your
su, sus- his, her, its	**su, sus-** their

The possessive adjective preceeds the noun to which it refers. The ending of the adjective reflects the number of the thing possessed: *mi casa, mis libros, nuestra casa, nuestros libros, su casa, sus libros,* etc.

Nuestro and *vuestro* reflect gender (masculine or feminine) as well as number of the object possessed (not of the owner): *nuestras amigas, vuestros amigos,* etc. Since *su* and *sus* can have multiple meanings ("your," formal, singular and plural; "his"; "her"; "its"; "their," masculine or feminine), another structure is sometimes used instead for clarification: definite article + noun + *de* + possessor (subject pronoun).

su libro = el libro de...

> usted
> él
> ella
> Juan
> ustedes
> ellos
> ellas
> Juan y María

Demonstrative Adjectives and Pronouns

this/these	that/those (nearby)	that/those (over there)
este/estos	**ese/esos**	**aquel/aquellos**
esta/estas	**esa/esas**	**aquella/aquellas**

When used as adjectives, the demonstratives precede the noun and must agree in number and gender with the noun they describe: *este hotel, esa comida, aquellos hombres,* etc.

When used as a pronoun ("this one," "that one," "these," "those," etc.), the demonstratives have accent marks: *este libro y ése* ("this book and that one"); *esta puerta y ésa* ("this door and that one"), etc.

The difference between *ese* and *aquel* is one of relative distance. The thing farthest away from the speaker is *aquel*, whereas *ese* implies that it is a bit closer.

In addition to the demonstrative adjectives, the demonstrative pronouns also include a series of neutral forms. These forms do not carry an accent mark.

esto　　　　**eso**　　　　　　**aquello**

LEARN TO SPEAK SPANISH

They refer to either something that has not being identified or to abstract ideas.

For example:
¿Qué es <u>esto</u>? . . . . What is <u>this</u>?

In this instance, the neutral form is used because the speaker does not recognize the object to which s/he is referring.

<u>Eso</u> es una buena idea. . . . .<u>That</u>'s a good idea.

In this instance, "*eso*" refers to an abstract idea, and therefore the neutral form is used.

Formation of Adverbs

Just as one can identify English adverbs by their ending in "-ly" ("quickly", "fairly"), one can recognize many Spanish adverbs by their *"-mente"* ending. To form these adverbs, the ending *"-mente"* is added to the feminine form of a descriptive adjective:

Masculine Adjective	Feminine Adjective	Adverb
claro	**clara**	**clara<u>mente</u>** (clearly)
triste	**triste**	**triste<u>mente</u>** (sadly)
fácil	**fácil**	**fácil<u>mente</u>** (happily)

If the feminine form of the adjective carries a written accent mark, it must be kept in its adverbial form, as in the last example above.

Placement of Adverbs

The placement of adverbs in Spanish does not follow any steadfast rule, though they are usually placed after the verb they modify:

Examples:
Él escribe <u>rápidamente</u>. . . . . .He writes <u>quickly</u>.
Ella lo aprende <u>fácilmente</u>. . . . . .She learns it <u>easily</u>.

Many adverbs that refer to time and space, however, come at the beginning of the sentence.

<u>Aquí</u> no hay queso. . . . . .There is no cheese <u>here</u>.
<u>Hoy</u> voy a la playa. . . . . .I'm going to the beach <u>today</u>.

Mucho, Muy, and Poco

Mucho ("a lot," "many") and *poco* ("a few," "few") can be either adjectives or adverbs. An adjective modifies a noun, while an adverb usually modifies a verb, adjective, or another adverb. When they are adjectives, they precede the noun, and they have four forms reflecting number and gender: *mucho, mucha, muchos, muchas.* For example, *mucha (poca) cerveza, muchos (pocos) hombres, mucho (poco) dinero, muchas (pocas) amigas.* To express very large or small amounts of something, use *muchísimo* and *poquísimo.*

When *mucho* and *poco* are adverbs, they do not change form. They generally follow the verb, and mean "very much" or "very little": *Roberto trabaja mucho (poco).*

Muy is an adverb. It means "very": *muy rápido, muy interestante, muy bien.* Never use *muy* with *mucho.* To express very large or very small amounts of something, use *muchísimo/a and poquísimo/a.*

Comparisons of Equality

To compare nouns, adjectives, or adverbs that are equal ("as ... as"; "as much/many ... as") use these formulas:

tan + adjective or adverb + *como*
Eduardo es tan inteligente como Roberto.
Eduardo is as intelligent as Roberto.

Eduardo habla tan rápido como Roberto.
Eduardo speaks as quickly as Roberto.

tanto/a/os/as + noun + *como*
Tengo tanto dinero como tú.
I have as much money as you.
Bebo tanta cerveza como tú.
I drink as much beer as you.
Ella tiene tantos amigos como yo.
She has as many friends as I.
Ella tiene tantas amigas como yo.
She has as many friends (f.) as I.

Notice that *tanto* will agree in number and gender with the noun it describes: *tantas horas, tantos días,* etc.

Comparisons of Inequality

When you are comparing things that are not equal ("more than"; "less than," "better than," etc.), use these formulas:

más + adjective/adverb/noun + que = more than
menos + adjective/adverb/noun + que = less than

Roberto es más inteligente que Pablo.
Roberto is more intelligent than Pablo.
Pablo es menos inteligente que Roberto.
Pablo is less intelligent than Roberto.

Roberto habla más rápido que Pablo.
Roberto speaks more quickly than Pablo.
Pablo habla menos rápido que Roberto.
Pablo speaks less rapidly than Roberto.

Roberto tiene más amigos que Pablo.
Roberto has more friends than Pablo.
Pablo tiene menos amigos que Roberto.
Pablo has less (fewer) friends than Roberto.

Some comparison forms are irregular and must be memorized.

bueno/bien .... **mejor-** better
malo/mal .... **peor-** worse
joven .... **menor-** younger
viejo .... **mayor-** older

Interrogative Words

¿Cómo? (How, what?)
¿Cómo estás? (How are you?)
¿Cómo te llamas? (What is your name?)
¿Dónde? (Where?)
¿Dónde está el hotel? (Where is the hotel?)
¿Qué? (What?)
¿Qué hora es? (What time is it?)
¿Qué es esto? (What is this?)
¿Qué necesita usted? (What do you need?)
¿Cuánto? ¿Cuánta? (How much?)

¿**Cuántos?** ¿**Cuántas?** (How many?)
¿**Cuántos días?** (How many days?)
¿**Cuánto dinero necesitas?** (How much money do you need?)
¿**Cuántas cervezas quieres comprar?** (How many beers do you want to buy?)
¿**Cuántas personas?** (How many people?)
¿**Cuándo?** (When?)
¿**Cuándo llegas?** (When do you arrive?)
¿**Quién?** ¿**Quiénes?** (Who?)
¿**Quién es ella?** (Who is she?)
¿**Quiénes son ellos?** (Who are they?)

Negative and Indefinite Words

nada	.nothing	**algo**	.something
nadie	.no one	**alguien**	.someone
ningún	.no, none	**algún**	.some, any
ninguno/a	.no, none	**alguno/a/os/as**	.some, any
nunca	.never	**siempre**	.always
tampoco	.neither	**también**	.also
ni... ni	.neither nor	**o... o**	.either or

Spanish uses a double negative with *no* preceding the verb, and a negative word following the verb: *No conozco a nadie* (literally, "I don't know no one"); *No trabajo nunca*; *No hablo francés tampoco*; *No tengo nada,* etc. In addition, to answer a "yes-no" question in the negative, you would use another *no*: *¿Necesita usted algo?*— *No, no necesito nada.*

Note that before a masculine singular noun, *ninguno* and *alguno* drop the final *-o* and take a written accent on the *u*: *ningún taxi, algún restaurante,* but *ninguna cajera, de ninguna manera* ("no way").

VERBS
Present Tense Indicative: Regular Verbs

In Spanish, all infinitive forms of verbs end in -*ar*, -*er*, or -*ir*. The stem of the verb is the infinitive form less the -*ar*, -*er*, or -*ir* ending. All regular verbs are conjugated in the present tense of the indicative by adding the following personal endings to the stem of the verb:

-*ar* verbs		-*er* verbs	
yo	-o	yo	-o
tú	-as	tú	-es
él, ella, Ud.	-a	él, ella, Ud.	-e
nosotros/as	-amos	nosotros/as	-emos
vosotros/as	-áis	vosotros/as	-éis
ellos, ellas, Uds.	-an	ellos, ellas, Uds.	-en

-*ir* verbs	
yo	-o
tú	-es
él, ella, Ud	-e
nosotros/as	-imos
vosotros/as	-ís
ellos, ellas, Uds.	-en

SAMPLE CONJUGATIONS

Hablar (to speak)	**Comer** (to eat)	**Vivir** (to live)
stem: **habl-**	stem: **com-**	stem: **viv-**
hablo	como	vivo
hablas	comes	vives
habla	come	vive
hablamos	comemos	vivimos
habláis	coméis	vivís
hablan	comen	viven

Common Regular Verbs

Some common regular verbs ending in -*ar* are:
> *bailar* ("to dance"), *buscar* ("to look for"), *cambiar* ("to change," "to exchange"), *comprar* ("to buy"), *desear* ("to want"), *estudiar* ("to study"), *hablar* ("to speak"), *llegar* ("to arrive"), *necesitar* ("to need"), *pagar* ("to pay for"), *preguntar* ("to ask"), *regresar* ("to return"), *tomar* ("to take," "to drink"), *trabajar* ("to work").

Some common regular verbs ending in -*er* are:
> *aprender* ("to learn"), *beber* ("to drink"), *comer* ("to eat"), *comprender* ("to understand"), *creer* ("to think"), *leer* ("to read").

Some common regular verbs ending in -*ir* are:
> *abrir* ("to open"), *asistir* ("to attend"), *escribir* ("to write"), *insistir* ("to insist"), *recibir* ("to receive"), *vivir* ("to live").

All of these verbs will follow the patterns you have just learned.

Stem-Changing Verbs

Some verbs do not follow the pattern of regular present tense verbs, and must be memorized. For example, the *yo* forms of *salir, tener,* and *venir* are irregular: *salgo*, *tengo*, and *vengo*. In addition, for other forms of *tener* and *venir* as well as *preferir* and *querer*, when the stem vowel -*e*- is stressed, it becomes *ie: tienes, vienes, prefieres, quieres,* and so on. In the same manner, the stem vowel -*o*- in *poder* becomes *ue* when stressed: *puedes.* In vocabulary lists, these changes are listed in parentheses beside the infinitive verb: preferir (ie); *poder (ue),* and so on.

TENER (to have)		**QUERER** (to want)	
tengo	tenemos	quiero	queremos
tienes	tenéis	quieres	queréis
tiene	tienen	quiere	quieren

PODER (to be able)		**VENIR** (to come)	
puedo	podemos	vengo	venimos
puedes	podéis	vienes	venís
puede	pueden	viene	vienen

PREFERIR (to prefer)		**SALIR** (to leave)	
prefiero	preferimos	salgo	salimos
prefieres	preferís	sales	salís
prefiere	prefieren	sale	salen

Stem-Changing Verbs: Present Tense

Many verbs change the stem vowel to a dipthong in the present tense. They are conjugated as follows:

e > ie		o or u > ue	
PENSAR (to think)		**VOLVER** (to return)	
pienso	pensamos	vuelvo	volvemos
piensas	pensáis	vuelves	volvéis
piensa	piensan	vuelve	vuelven

e > i (ir verbs only)	
PEDIR (to ask for)	
pido	pedimos
pides	pedís
pide	piden

Notice that the *nosotros* and *vosotros* forms of the verbs do not have stem changes, whereas the others do.

More Stem-Changing Verbs

e > ie	o or u > ue	e > i
cerrar (to close)	**almorzar** (to eat lunch)	**pedir** (to ask for)
empezar (to begin)	**dormir** (to sleep)	**servir** (to serve)
pensar (to think)	**jugar** (to play (games))	
perder (to lose)	**poder** (to be able)	
preferir (to prefer)	**volver** (to return)	
querer (to want)		

Irregular Verbs in the Present Tense

These verbs are commonly used and, since they do not follow the pattern you have learned for regular verbs, they must be memorized.

IR (to go)	**voy**	**vamos**	**vas**	**vais**	**va**	**van**
DAR (to give)	**doy**	**damos**	**das**	**dais**	**da**	**dan**
TRAER (to bring)	**traigo**	**traemos**	**traes**	**traéis**	**trae**	**traen**
PONER (to put)	**pongo**	**ponemos**	**pones**	**ponéis**	**pone**	**ponen**
DECIR (to tell, say)	**digo**	**decimos**	**dices**	**decís**	**dice**	**dicen**
OIR (to hear)	**oigo**	**oímos**	**oyes**	**oís**	**oye**	**oyen**

Ser and *Estar* (to be)

Spanish has two verbs that mean "to be": *ser* and *estar*. Both are irregular in the present tense indicative, and their forms must be memorized.

SER . . . . .ESTAR
soy . . . .**estoy**
eres . . . .**estás**
es . . . .**está**
somos . . . .**estamos**
sois . . . .**estáis**
son . . . .**están**

Notice that many forms of *estar* have written accent marks.

Some Uses of *Ser* and *Estar*

Ser and *estar* have numerous uses which you will learn throughout your Spanish studies. *Ser* can be used with many impersonal expressions, such as *es importante, es interesante, es ridículo*. In addition, some of the common uses of *ser* include:

— to identify a person or a thing
Soy el secretario de la señora Garza.

— to tell time, the day of the week or the date
Hoy es domingo. Es el diez de mayo. Son las nueve de la mañana.

— to express national origin
Nosotros somos de México, pero ellos son de Uruguay.

— to describe the characteristics or traits of a person or thing
María es inteligente. Yo soy tímido. El restaurante es grande, pero bueno.

LEARN TO SPEAK SPANISH

— to tell what someone does for a living
Antonia es profesora y yo soy ingeniera.

Some comon uses of the verb *estar* are:

— to tell location of a person or thing
Estoy en el restaurante.

— to desribe the emotional or physical condition or someone or something
Octavio y Juan están ocupados. Alicia está bien, pero yo estoy mal.

The Verb *Gustar*

The verb *gustar* literally means "to be pleasing to" but it is most commonly translated as "to like" in English. "I like this hotel" becomes *Me gusta este hotel* (literally, "This hotel is pleasing to me"). To talk about what other people like or dislike, use the appropriate indirect object pronoun form in front of the verb. To whom is something pleasing?

me (to me) . . . .**nos** (to us)
te (to you [informal]) . . . .**os** (to you [informal])
le (to you [formal], to him, to her) . . . .**les** (to you [formal], to him, to her)

When you are describing your own likes and dislikes, use the indirect object pronoun me before the verb. Generally, *gustar* is used in just two ways: *gusta* (for one thing that is pleasing) or *gustan* (for more than one thing that is pleasing): *Me gusta el restaurante; Me gustan los tacos.* To say that you don't like something, place a *no* in front of the indirect object pronoun: *No me gusta el hotel; No me gustan las enchiladas.* Avoid using *gustar* to talk about liking people, as it has sexual connotations in some regions.

What is pleasing? *¿El hotel? Me gusta el hotel, Te gusta el hotel, Le gusta el hotel, Nos gusta el hotel, Os gusta el hotel, Les gusta el hotel. ¿Los tacos? Me gustan los tacos, Te gustan los tacos, Le gustan los tacos, Nos gustan los tacos, Os gustan los tacos, Les gustan los tacos.* Notice that the verb form, *gusta* or *gustan*, agrees in singular or plural with its grammatical subject, the thing or things that are pleasing, not with the person that is pleased. Finally, when a verb follows *gustar*, it will be in the infinitive: *Me gusta comer tacos.*

Verbs Like *Gustar*

Several verbs in Spanish follow the same pattern as the verb gustar:

doler (ue)- to hurt	**importar**- to be important
encantar- to like a lot	**interesar**- to be of interest
faltar- to be lacking	**molestar**- to bother, annoy
fascinar- to fascinate	**parecer**- to seem, appear
fastidiar- to upset, bother	**preocupar**- to worry (someone)
hacer falta- to be lacking	**quedar**- to remain, be left

(A mí) Me molestan los embotellamientos de tráfico.
Traffic jams bother me.

(A ti) ¿Te interesan estos libros?
Do these books interest you?

(A usted) Le fascinan las representaciones folklóricas.
The folkloric shows fascinate you.

(A Elena) Le encanta el pescado.
She likes fish a lot.

(A nosotras) No nos queda mucho tiempo.
We don't have much time left.

(A vosotros) ¿Os preocupa la idea?
Does the idea worry you?

(A ustedes) Les faltan 30,000 pesos.
They lack 30,000 pesos.

(A ellas) Les duele la cabeza.
They have headaces.

Saber vs. *Conocer*

Both *saber* and *conocer* mean "to know," but they are not used interchangeably.
Saber is "to know" information *(No sé el número de teléfono; ¿Sabe usted dónde está el restaurante?)*, or "to know how" to do something *(No sabemos conducir)*.
Conocer is "to know" a person *(Conozco a la Sra. García; ¿Conoces a mi hermana?)*, or "to be familiar with" a place or a thing *(No conocen la ciudad)*.
Both verbs are irregular and must be memorized.

LEARN TO SPEAK SPANISH

SABER	CONOCER
sé	conozco
sabes	conoces
sabe	conoce
sabemos	conocemos
sabéis	conocéis
saben	conocen

Pedir vs. *Preguntar*

Both *pedir* and *preguntar* mean "to ask," but they are not interchangeable.
Preguntar means "to ask a question": *Roberto le pregunta dónde está la oficina*
("Roberto asks her where the office is"). *Pedir* means "to ask for something," and is
also used to mean "to order" (in a restaurant): *Roberto le pide información*
("Roberto asks her for information"). *Roberto pide los tacos* ("Roberto orders
tacos").

Pedir is slightly irregular, and should be memorized.
    PEDIR (to ask for, to order)
    pido
    pedimos
    pides
    pedís
    pide
    piden

Hacer (to do, make)

The verb *hacer* is irregular in the present tense. You must memorize it.

HACER (to make, to do)	**hago**	**hacemos**	**haces**
	hacéis	**hace**	**hacen**

The word "do" in English questions such as "Do you speak Spanish?" is not
translated into Spanish: *¿Habla usted español?* The verb *hacer* is used to ask the
question *¿Qué hace usted?* ("What are you doing?"), but the answer to this question
generally involves a verb other than *hacer: Leo un libro* ("I'm reading a book"), etc.
Answer with *hacer* only when you are actually making something: *Hago un pastel*
("I'm making a cake").

The Meaning of Hay

Hay is an irregular form of the the verb *haber*. It means "there is" or "there are," and it is used to point out the existence or presence of someone or something:

Hay un restaurante bueno cerca de aquí.
There is a good restaurant close to here.

Hay muchos taxis en la calle.
There are many taxis in the street.

Hay cinco socios en la firma.
There are five partners in the firm.

Hay diez empleados en la oficina.
There are ten employees in the office.

When referring to the past, the verb form becomes *había* (imperfect) or sometimes *hubo*:

Había (Hubo) un restaurante bueno cerca de aquí.
There was a good restaurant close to here.

Había (Hubo) muchos taxis en la calle.
There were many taxis in the street.

Había (Hubo) cinco socios en la firma.
There were five partners in the firm.

Había (Hubo) diez empleados en la oficina.
There were ten employees in the office.

Note: *Hay*, *había*, and *hubo* point out the existence or presence of something. If you are pointing out the location of specific persons or things, use a form of *estar*:

Roberto está en casa.
Roberto is at home.

Silvia y Elena están en el mercado.
Silvia and Elena are at the market.

La carta está en la mesa.
The letter is on the table.

Los libros están en el suelo.
The books are on the floor.

Some Idioms with *Tener*

An idiom is an expression that cannot be translated literally from one language to another. A number of idioms in Spanish involve the verb *tener*, and must be memorized.

tener ...años	.to be ...years old
tener hambre	.to be hungry
tener sed	.to be thirsty
tener frío	.to be cold
tener calor	.to be hot
tener prisa	.to be in a hurry
tener sueño	.to be sleepy
tener razón	.to be right
no tener razón	.to be wrong
tener miedo (de)	.to be afraid of
tener ganas (de)	.to feel like (doing something)
tener que + infinitive	.to have to (do something)

Some Uses of *Hace*

The verb form *hace* is used in many weather expressions. These are idioms and should be memorized.

¿Qué tiempo hace?	.What's the weather like?
Hace buen tiempo.	.The weather is nice.
Hace mal tiempo.	.The weather is bad.
Hace frío.	.It's cold.
Hace calor.	.It's hot.
Hace viento.	.It's windy.
Hace sol.	.It's sunny.
Hace fresco.	.It's cool.

When used with a time expression and a verb in the present tense, *(desde) hace* means for a certain amount of time: *(Desde) Hace un mes estoy en México* ("I have been in Mexico for a month"). When used with the past tense, it means "ago": *Lo conocí hace seis años* ("I met him six years ago").

Reflexive Verbs and Pronouns

A number of verbs in Spanish are reflexive, and are always used with a reflexive pronoun. The pronoun form corresponds to, or reflects the subject (the person doing the action), and immediately precedes the conjugated verb.

MARCHARSE
(yo) me marcho	**(nostros/as) nos marchamos**
(tú) te marchas	**(vosotros/as) os marcháis**
(Ud., él, ella) se marcha	**(Uds., ellos, ellas) se marchan**

The reflexive pronouns can also be attached to infinitives: *Tengo que irme; to gerunds: Está bañándose;* and to affirmative commands: *Levántate.* With negative commands, the pronoun precedes the verb: *No te vayas.*

Common Reflexive Verbs

acostarse (ue)	.to go to bed
levantarse	.to get up
afeitarse	.to shave
llamarse	.to be named (called)
bañarse	.to take a bath
ponerse	.to put on (clothes)
despertarse (ie)	.to wake up
quitarse	.to take off (clothes)
divertirse (ie)	.to enjoy oneself
sentarse	.to sit down
dormirse (ue)	.to fall asleep
sentirse (ie)	.to feel
lavarse	.to wash (oneself)
vestirse (i)	.to get dressed

Notice that the infinitive always shows *-se* attached to the end of a reflexive verb. When you conjugate the verb, remember to make the pronoun form correspond to the person doing the action: *dormirse (ue) > me duermo, te duermes, se duerme, nos dormimos, os dormís, se duermen.*

The vowels in parentheses *(ue) (ie)*, etc. indicate that the verb has a stem change.

Reciprocal Actions

The plural reflexive pronouns *(nos, os, se)* can be used to express mutual or reciprocal actions, generally expressed in English as "each other".

Roberto y Thomas se saludan ("They greet each other"). *Elena y Thomas se escriben* ("They write to each other"). *Ustedes se quieren mucho* ("You all love each other a lot"). *Ustedes se conocen, ¿verdad?* ("You all know each other, don't you?"). *Vosotros os veis con frecuencia* ("You all see each other often"). *Nosotros nos conocemos hace años* ("We've know each other for years").

Present Progressive

The present progressive is formed in Spanish by using a conjugated form of the verb *estar* and a *gerund*. The *gerunds* are formed for verbs ending in *-ar* by adding *-ando* to the stem; for verbs ending in *-er* or *-ir*, add *-iendo* to the stem: *hablando, bailando, trabajando, comiendo, viviendo, diciendo,* etc. When an unstressed *-i-* occurs between two vowels, it becomes a *-y-*: *leer > leyendo; creer > creyendo,* etc.

Keep in mind that the present progressive is not as common in Spanish as it is in English. The simple present tense *(trabajo, estudio,* etc.) is used more frequently to indicate actions in progress.

Preterite of Regular Verbs

Spanish uses two tenses to describe past actions and events: the preterite and the imperfect. The preterite is used for actions that were completed in the past. The preterite endings are added to the stem of the infinitive *(habl-, com-, viv-)*. Notice the *-er* and *-ir* verbs have the same endings in the preterite.

-ar verbs	*-er* verbs	*-ir* verbs
HABLAR	COMER	VIVIR
hablé	**comí**	**viví**
hablaste	**comiste**	**viviste**
habló	**comió**	**vivió**
hablamos	**comimos**	**vivimos**
hablasteis	**comisteis**	**vivisteis**
hablaron	**comieron**	**vivieron**

Note: *Ver* has no accents in the preterite: *vi, viste, vio, vimos, visteis, vieron.*

Preterite of Irregular Verbs

There are many verbs that are irregular in the preterite. Their forms must be memorized.

DAR	IR	SER
di	fui	fui
diste	fuiste	fuiste
dio	fue	fue
dimos	fuimos	fuimos
disteis	fuisteis	fuisteis
dieron	fueron	fueron

The rest of the irregular verbs share the preterite endings *-e, -iste, -o, -imos, -isteis, -ieron.* Notice that none of the endings have accent marks. For these verbs you can learn the irregular preterite stem and use the appropriate endings. **Note:** The third person singular form of *hacer* has a spelling change of *c > z: hizo.* Also, the third person plural form of *decir* and *traer* does not use the *-i-* of the ending: *dijeron, trajeron.*

hacer > hic-	querer > quis-
estar > estuv-	saber > sup-
tener > tuv-	venir > vin-
poder > pud-	decir > dij-
poner > pus-	traer > traj-

Some Spelling Changes in the Preterite

Verbs that have stem changes in the present tense do not have the same change in the preterite. Verbs ending in *-ar* or *-er* have no stem change in the preterite: *pensar* (ie) > *pensé, pensaste, pensó, pensamos,* etc.; *volver* (ie) > *volví, volviste, volvió, volvimos,* etc.

Verbs ending in *-ir* do have a stem change in the preterite, but only in the third person singular and plural. This change is not always the same change as for the present tense. In vocabulary lists, stem changes for the preterite are listed in parentheses next to the stem change information for the present tense.

DORMIR (ue, u)	PEDIR (i, i)
dormí	pedí
dormiste	pediste
durmió	pidió
dormimos	pedimos

dormisteis	**pedisteis**
durmieron	**pidieron**

Verbs ending in *-car, -gar,* and *-zar* have a spelling change in the first person singular of the verb, where *c > qu, g > gu, and z > c.* A similar spelling change occurs for these verbs in the formal commands and in the present subjunctive.

buscar > busqué
pagar > pagué
empezar > empecé

Verbs ending in two unstressed vowels have a spelling change in the third person singular and plural.

creer > creyó, creyeron
leer > leyó, leyeron
caer > cayó, cayeron

Imperfect Tense

Spanish uses two tenses to describe past actions and events: the preterite and the imperfect. The imperfect is used to talk about actions or events that were in progress in the past, things that were habitual or customary, or that happened over a long period of time. It is also used to describe ongoing mental, physical, or emotional states in the past, and to tell time in the past.

-ar verbs	*-er* verbs	*-ir* verbs
HABLAR	COMER	VIVIR
hablaba	**comía**	**vivía**
hablabas	**comías**	**vivías**
hablaba	**comía**	**vivía**
hablábamos	**comíamos**	**vivíamos**
hablabais	**comíais**	**vivíais**
hablaban	**comían**	**vivían**

INSTALLING YOUR PROGRAM

1. Close all programs and dialog windows.

2. Insert the CD into your CD-ROM drive.

   Note: If the installation process doesn't begin, click the Windows® Start button and choose **Run.** Click **Browse,** and select your CD-ROM drive from the Look In list. Select **CDSETUP** (or **CDSETUP.EXE**) and click **Open.** If you do not see a file named **CDSETUP,** select **SETUP** or **(SETUP.EXE)** and click **Open.**

3. Follow the on-screen instructions to complete the installation.

4. A program group will be added to your **Start, Programs** menu. If it contains a **Readme** shortcut, please open it and follow its instructions.

   • Depending on your system, the program group may be inserted in alphabetical order or it may be added to the bottom of your list. If you do not see a program group on your **Start, Programs** menu, look on your desktop for a new shortcut.

Cosmi Corporation
1351 Charles Willard St.
Carson, CA 90746
www.cosmi.com

Cosmi Customer Service
support@cosmi.com
Phone: (310) 886-3510
Fax: (310) 886-3517

09.20.04

Only three verbs are irregular in the imperfect tense:

IR	SER	VER
iba	**era**	**veía**
ibas	**eras**	**veías**
iba	**era**	**veía**
íbamos	**éramos**	**veíamos**
ibais	**erais**	**veíais**
iban	**eran**	**veían**

There are no stem-changes in the imperfect tense. Verbs that are stem-changing in the present or preterite are conjugated like regular verbs in the imperfect: *volvía, jugaba, pensaba, perdía,* etc.

Preterite vs. Imperfect

The preterite is used to narrate completed actions in the past. Certain words like *ayer* ("yesterday"), *anoche* ("last night"), *el año pasado* ("last year"), and *la semana pasada* ("last week"), are associated with the preterite since they usually refer to specific events that are now completed.

The imperfect is used to narrate actions that were habitual or ongoing in the past. There is no reference to whether or not these things were ever completed, or whether they continue into the present time. Phrases like *siempre* ("always"), *frecuentemente* ("frequently"), and *todos los días* ("daily"), are often associated with the imperfect. The difference between the preterite and imperfect is often very subtle, and even native speakers will occasionally disagree about which form is correct. You should study examples and try to imitate native speakers when possible.

Past Participle

The past participle is formed in Spanish by adding *-ado* to the stem of regular *-ar* verbs, and *-ido* to the stem of regular *-er* or *-ir* verbs: *hablar > hablado; poder > podido; vivir > vivido,* etc.

The past participle can often be used as an adjective (usually with the verb *estar*). Then, it has four forms, reflecting the number and gender of the noun it describes:

El precio está confirmado. . . . . .The price is confirmed.
La tarifa está confirmada. . . . . .The fare is confirmed.
Los fondos están confirmados. . . . . .The funds are confirmed.
Las reservaciones están confirmadas. . . . .The reservations are confirmed.

LEARN TO SPEAK SPANISH

The past participle can also be used with the verb *ser* to construct the passive voice: **La comida fue preparada por mamá** ("The food was prepared by Mom"). Again, the past participle reflects number and gender of the noun it describes. The passive construction with *ser* + past participle is not as common in Spanish as it is in English. The active voice should be used whenever possible: *Mamá preparó la comida* ("Mom made the food").

Some Irregular Past Participles

The following verbs have irregular past participles which must be memorized.

abrir	.abierto	morir	.muerto
decir	.dicho	poner	.puesto
cubrir	.cubierto	resolver	.resuelto
descubrir	.descubierto	romper	.roto
escribir	.escrito	ver	.visto
hacer	.hecho	volver	.vuelto

An accent mark is added to the past participle of *-er* and *-ir* verbs with stems ending in a vowel: *caer > caído, creer > creído, leer > leído, oír > oído, traer > traído,* etc.

Present Perfect Tense

The present perfect is constructed by using a conjugated form of the irregular verb haber with the past participle.

he comido	.hemos comido
has comido	.habéis comido
ha comido	.han comido

The past participle does not change form when it is used in the present perfect tense. For example; *Ella ha comido, nosotros hemos comido, ustedes han comido,* etc. Like its English counterpart, the present perfect tense is used to refer to the past. In the affirmative, it refers to an action that has already taken place; *Elena ha llegado* ("Elena has arrived"). In the negative, it refers to something that has not happened yet; *No ha llegado* ("She hasn't arrived yet").

Informal *Tú* Commands

Affirmative *tú* commands have the same form as the third person singular
(él, ella, usted) of the present indicative: *Habla (tú)*; *Cierra (tú) la ventana;
Limpia (tú) los dormitorios; Come (tú) las verduras; Trae (tú) los regalos;
Corre (tú) en el parque.*

Negative *tú* commands have the same form as the *tú* form of the present subjunctive:
*No hables (tú); No cierres (tú) la ventana; No limpies (tú) los dormitorios;
No comas (tú) los chocolates; No traigas (tú) los regalos; No corras (tú) en
el parque.*

Direct, indirect and reflexive pronouns are attached to affirmative commands:
tráeme, explícame, déjalo, levántate, siéntate, etc.

Direct, indirect, and reflexive pronouns precede a negative tú command: *no me
traigas, no me expliques, no lo dejes, no te levantes, no te sientes,* etc.

Irregular *Tú* Commands

There are only a few irregular *tú* commands, and these are irregular only in the
affirmative command form. The negative command forms are the same as the *tú*
form of the present subjunctive.

decir: di, no digas	**salir: sal, no salgas**
hacer: haz, no hagas	**ser: sé, no seas**
ir: ve, no vayas	**tener: ten, no tengas**
poner: pon, no pongas	**venir: ven, no vengas**

Formal Commands

When you are directly addressing a person or persons that you would normally
address as *usted* or *ustedes*, give formal commands by taking the *yo* form of the
present indicative tense and changing the ending of *-ar* verbs to *-e* for singular
(usted) commands, or *-en* for plural *(ustedes)* commands and changing the ending
of *-er/-ir* verbs to *-a* or *-an*. Because you are working from the *yo* form of the
present indicative, the formal commands reflect the irregularities you find in irregular
and stem-changing verbs.

Regular Verbs
-AR -ER/-IR

buscar > busque, busquen*	**comer > coma, coman**
dejar > deje, dejen	**insistir > insista, insistan**

hablar > hable, hablen	**leer > lea, lean**
llamar > llame, llamen	**vivir > viva, vivan**

Verbs with Irregular *yo* Forms

conocer (conozco)>conozca, conozcan	**salir (salgo)>salga, salgan**
decir (digo)>diga, digan	**tener (tengo) >tenga, tengan**
oír (oigo)>oiga, oigan	**traer (traigo)>traiga, traigan**
poner (pongo)>ponga, pongan	**venir (vengo)>venga, vengan**

Stem-Changing Verbs

almorzar (ue) > almuerce, almuercen*	**pedir (i) > pida, pidan**
cerrar (ie) > cierre, cierren	**perder (ie) > pierda, pierdan**
empezar (ie) > empiece, empiecen	**servir (i) > sirva, sirvan**
jugar (ue) > juegue, jueguen*	**volver (ue) > vuelva, vuelvan**

* A spelling change is necessary to preserve the sound of the infinitives that end in -*car, -gar, and -zar: c > qu, g > gu, and z > c.*

A few verbs have irregular command forms and must be memorized:

dar > dé, den	saber > sepa, sepan
estar > esté, estén	ser > sea, sean
ir > vaya, vayan	

How to Talk About the Future

There are many ways you can talk about the future in Spanish. The easiest is to use an adverbial phrase indicating a future time (such as *mañana, más tarde, luego, a la(s)* + time, and so on) with the present tense of the verb: *mañana voy al aeropuerto* ("tomorrow I'm going to the airport"); *luego hablamos por teléfono* ("we'll talk on the telephone later"); *a las cinco nos encontramos en la oficina de correos* ("at five o'clock we'll meet at the post office").

Another way to talk about the future is with the future tense. The future tense in Spanish is formed by adding the endings -*é, -ás, -á, -emos, -éis, -án* to the entire infinitive.

Study these examples:

-*ar* verbs	-*er* verbs	-*ir* verbs
HABLAR	COMER	VIVIR
hablaré	**comeré**	**viviré**
hablarás	**comerás**	**vivirás**
hablará	**comerá**	**vivirá**
hablaremos	**comeremos**	**viviremos**
hablaréis	**comeréis**	**viviréis**
hablarán	**comerán**	**vivirán**

Another very common way to talk about the future is to use the verb *ir* in a conjugated form in the present tense, followed by the preposition a and an infinitive: *voy a comer* ("I am going to eat"; "I will eat"); *vas a comer, va a comer, vamos a comer, vais a comer, van a comer,* etc. This structure is especially common in spoken Spanish.

Some Irregular Verbs in the Future Tense

DECIR > dir-
   diré, dirás, dirá, diremos, diréis, dirán
HABER > habr-
   habré, habrás, habrá, habremos, habréis, habrán
HACER > har-
   haré, harás, hará, haremos, haréis, harán
PODER > podr-
   podré, podrás, podrá, podremos, podréis, podrán
QUERER > querr-
   querré, querrás, querrá, querremos, querréis, querrán
SABER > sabr-
   sabré, sabrás, sabrá, sabremos, sabréis, sabrán
PONER > pondr-
   pondré, pondrás, pondrá, pondremos, pondréis, pondrán
SALIR > saldr-
   saldré, saldrás, saldrá, saldremos, saldréis, saldrán
TENER > tendr-
   tendré, tendrás, tendrá, tendremos, tendréis, tendrán
VENIR > vendre-
   vendré, vendrás, vendrá, vendremos, vendréis, vendrán

Conditional Tense

Like the future tense, the conditional is formed by adding endings (*-ía, -ías, -ía, -íamos, -íais, -ían*) to the entire infinitive. Do not confuse the conditional forms of *-er* and *-ir* verbs with the imperfect. The endings for the latter are added to the stem, not to the infinitive.

-ar verbs	*-er* verbs	*-ir* verbs
HABLAR	COMER	VIVIR
hablaría	**comería**	**viviría**
hablarías	**comerías**	**vivirías**
hablaría	**comería**	**viviría**
hablaríamos	**comeríamos**	**viviríamos**
hablaríais	**comeríais**	**viviríais**
hablarían	**comerían**	**vivirían**

The conditional is used to talk about things that would happen under certain circumstances: *Un permanente le quedaría bien* ("A permanent would look good on you"), or to make polite requests; *Me gustaría [pedir] el pescado* ("I would like [to order] the fish").

Some Irregular Verbs in the Conditional Tense

DECIR > dir-
diría, dirías, diría, diríamos, diríais, dirían

HABER > habr-
habría, habrías, habría, habríamos, habríais, habrían

HACER > har-
haría, harías, haría, haríamos, haríais, harían

PODER > podr-
podría, podrías, podría, podríamos, podríais, podrían

QUERER > querr-
querría, querrías, querría, querríamos, querríais, querrían

SABER > sabr-
sabría, sabrías, sabría, sabríamos, sabríais, sabrían

PONER > pondr-
pondría, pondrías, pondría, pondríamos, pondríais, pondrían

SALIR > *saldr-*
saldría, saldrías, saldría, saldríamos, saldríais, saldrían

TENER > *tendr-*
tendría, tendrías, tendría, tendríamos, tendríais, tendrían

VENIR > vendre-
vendría, vendrías, vendría, vendríamos, vendríais, vendrían

Formation of the Present Subjunctive

To form the present subjunctive of most verbs, add the personal endings of the present subjunctive to the *yo* form of the present indicative minus the *-o* ending. For the subjunctive, *-ar* verb endings are *-e, -es, -e, -emos, -éis, -en,* and *-er / -ir* verb endings are *-a, -as, -a, -amos, -áis, -an.* (Notice that the third person forms [*él/ella/usted and ellos/ellas/ustedes*] of regular verbs in the subjunctive are the same forms used in formal commands.)

-ar verbs		*-er* verbs	
HABLAR		COMER	
hable	**hablemos**	**coma**	**comamos**
hables	**habléis**	**comas**	**comáis**
hable	**hablen**	**coma**	**coman**

-ir verbs
VIVIR
viva . . . . **vivamos**
vivas . . . . **viváis**
viva . . . . **vivan**

Since the form of the present subjunctive is taken from the yo form of the present indicative, stem-changing verbs and verbs that are irregular in the *yo* form have the same irregularity in the present subjunctive. In addition, verbs ending in *-car, -gar,* and *-zar* have the same spelling change as in formal commands: *c > qu,   g > gu, and z > c.*

The verbs that are irregular for the formal commands are also irregular for the present subjunctive. These forms must be memorized.

Spelling Changes in the Present Subjunctive

In the present subjunctive, the -ar and -er stem-changing verbs have the same pattern of stem changes as in the present indicative, only the endings are different.

PENSAR	VOLVER	DORMIR	PREFERIR
(ie)	*(ue)*	*(ue, u)*	*(ie, i)*
piense	**vuelva**	**duerma**	**prefiera**
pienses	**vuelvas**	**duermas**	**prefieras**
piense	**vuelva**	**duerma**	**prefiera**
pensemos	**volvamos**	**durmamos**	**prefiramos**
penséis	**volváis**	**durmáis**	**prefiráis**
piensen	**vuelvan**	**duerman**	**prefieran**

-*Ir* stem-changing verbs have a slightly different pattern in the subjunctive than in the present indicative. These are the same verbs that have a different stem change in the third person form of the preterite. The same stem change seen in the preterite is seen in the subjunctive in the *nosotros*/as and *vosotros*/as forms.

Verbs ending in -*car, -gar,* and -*zar* have a spelling change in all forms of the present subjunctive, with *c > qu, g > gu, and z > c.*

BUSCAR	PAGAR	EMPEZAR
busque	**pague**	**empiece**
busques	**pagues**	**empieces**
busque	**pague**	**empiece**
busquemos	**paguemos**	**empecemos**
busquéis	**paguéis**	**empecéis**
busquen	**paguen**	**empiecen**

Present Subjunctive of Irregular Verbs

These verbs are irregular in the present subjuntive and must be memorized:

DAR		ESTAR	
dé	**demos**	**esté**	**estemos**
des	**deis**	**estés**	**estéis**
dé	**den**	**esté**	**estén**

HABER		SABER	
haya	**hayamos**	**sepa**	**sepamos**
hayas	**hayáis**	**sepas**	**sepáis**
haya	**hayan**	**sepa**	**sepan**

IR	
vaya	**vayamos**
vayas	**vayáis**
vaya	**vayan**

Subjunctive After Impersonal Expressions

After impersonal expressions that indicate a willing, wish, command, preference, desire, necessity, opinion, etc. on the part of the speaker that another person do (or not do) something, the subjunctive is used in the dependent clause, after the word que:

Es importante que usted hable con la directora.
It's important that you speak with the director.

Es necesario que Elena tome un taxi.
It's necessary that Elena take a taxi.

¡Es terrible que no sepas hablar español!
It's terrible that you don't know how to speak Spanish!

Es posible que sea el efecto de la comida.
It's possible that it is the effect of the food.

No es preciso que usted tome medicina especial.
It's not necessary for you to take special medicine.

However, if the expression does not reflect the desire to influence a specific person to do something, but instead is a statement that people in general should do something, then the infinitive (*-ar, -er, -ir* forms), and not the subjunctive, is used.

Es necesario evitar el alcohol.
It's necessary to avoid alchohol.

Es preferible ir en autobús.
It's preferable to go by bus.

Es posible comprar comida aquí.
It's possible to buy food here.

Subjunctive After Verbs of Emotion

The subjunctive is used after certain expressions of emotion, when the speaker shows emotion about the actions of another person, as in *Me alegro de que estés aquí* ("I'm glad that you're here"). The subjunctive is also used after impersonal expressions of emotion, as in *Es una lástima que no puedas acompañarnos* ("It's a pity that you can't come with us").

You should recognize these expressions as some that will require the use of the subjunctive in the subordinate clause, after the word *que*: *alegrarse*("to be glad"), *esperar* ("to hope"), *sentir* ("to regret"), *temer* ("to be afraid"), *asombrarse* ("to be surprised"), *sorprenderse* ("to surprise"), *enfadarse* ("to be angry"), *enojarse* ("to be angry"), *es una lástima* ("it's a pity"), *es triste* ("it's sad"), *es escandaloso* ("it's scandalous"), *es terrible* ("it's terrible"), and so forth.

Subjunctive After Verbs of Willing

One of the most common uses of the subjunctive is after verbs of willing, such as *querer* ("to want"), *desear* ("to want"), *insistir en* ("to insist on"), *mandar* ("to order"), *preferir* ("to prefer"), *prohibir* ("to prohibit"), *recomendar* ("to recommend"), *decir* ("to tell" someone to do something), *pedir* ("to ask" someone to do something), and *permitir* ("to permit"). Notice that in the examples of the use of the subjunctive with the verbs of willing in the settings and dialogues, there is one person speaking who wants another person to do something. That is, there must be a change of subject in order to use the subjunctive—one subject wants to influence the other subject to do something. *Thomas quiere que la operadora llame...; Thomas quiere que la secretaria le indique...; Thomas quiere que el camarero le traiga...*, etc. The subjunctive is used after the conjunction que in the subordinate clause of the sentence. If there is no change of subject, the subjunctive is not used: *Thomas quiere comer; Thomas quiere llamar; Thomas quiere encontrar...; etc.*

Subjunctive in Adverbial Clauses

If an action has not yet occurred, a native speaker of Spanish will use the subjunctive after certain adverbial clauses such as: *tan pronto como* ("as soon as"), *cuando* ("when"), *después de que* ("after"), *en cuanto* ("as soon as"), *hasta que* ("until"), and *mientras* ("while," "as long as").

Podemos hablar del tema cuando usted llegue (you haven't arrived yet).

Puedo quedarme en un hotel mientras esté en México (for however long I am in Mexico — I haven't left yet).

Elena viene tan pronto como yo encuentre un apartamento
(I haven't found an apartment yet).

If the action has already taken place and there is therefore no doubt about its outcome, the subjunctive is not used: **Cuando estuve en Acapulco, fui a la playa** (I went to Acapulco in the past).

Subjunctive in Expressions of Doubt

The subjunctive is used after expressions of doubt or uncertainty: *dudar* ("to doubt"), *no creer* ("not to believe"), *no estar seguro/a* ("not to be sure"), *no es verdad* ("it's not true"), *es dudoso* ("it's doubtful"), *no es cierto* ("it's uncertain"), etc. As always, the subjunctive will be used after the word que in the subordinate clause of the sentence: *Dudo que pueda llegar antes de las nueve; No creo que el viaje sea largo; Es dudoso que la casa esté amueblada; No es cierto que tengan pescado en el mercado.*

If there is no doubt or uncertainty in the mind of the speaker, then the indicative is used: *Es cierto que mis padres vienen para Navidad; No hay duda de que sus nietos quieren verlos; Creo que van a estar aquí dos semanas.*

Note: *Creo que* and *no dudo que* are expressions of certainty, and thus require the indicative in the subordinate clause. *No creo que* and *dudo que* are expressions of doubt that call for the subjunctive in the subordinate clause.

PREPOSITIONS
Some Useful Prepositions

cerca de (near, close to)	**entre** (between)
lejos de (far, far from)	**durante** (during)
antes de (before)	**a la izquierda de** (to the left of)
después de (after)	**a la derecha de** (to the right of)
encima de (on top of)	**frente a** (facing)
debajo de (below)	**en frente de** (in front of)
delante de (in front of)	**detrás de** (behind)

In Spanish, the pronouns that follow prepositions are the same as the subject pronouns, except for first and second person singular forms: *mí, ti. Es para mí, es para ti, es para ella, es para ustedes,* etc. One exception to this is the expression "between you and me," *entre tú y yo.* The forms *conmigo* ("with me") and *contigo* ("with you" informal singular) are irregular and must be memorized.

Some Verbs that Require Prepositions

1. These verbs are followed by the preposition *a*.

aprender a (to learn to)	**enseñar a** (to teach to)
ayudar a (to help)	**invitar a** (to invite to)
comenzar a (to begin to)	**ir a** (to go to)
empezar a (to begin to)	**volver a** (to return to)

2. These verbs are followed by *de*.

acabar de (to just finish)	**olvidarse de** (to forget)
acordarse de (to remember)	**tener ganas de** (to feel like)
dejar de (to stop)	**tratar de** (to try to)

3. *Insistir* ("to insist") is followed by *en*, and will call for the subjunctive in the subordinate clause if there is a change of subject.

4. *Pensar* ("to think") can be followed by *en* or *de*, depending on the meaning intended: *Pienso en ti* ("I'm thinking about you" ["You're on my mind"]). *¿Qué piensas de ella?* ("What do you think about her?" ["What is your reaction," "your feeling about her?"]).

Note: The prepositions are used only when the grammatical object follows the verb. If no object follows, then no preposition is used: *¿Me ayudas a limpiar las ventanas? Sí, te ayudo.*

Some Uses of *Para*

Para is used to express the following:

to, in order to—**Trabajo para ganar plata.**

destined for, to be given to—**El libro es para ti.**

for (by a specific time)—**Estudien esta lección para mañana.**

for, in the direction of, toward—**Salimos para Acapulco.**

to be used for/by—**Es un hotel para turistas.**

for (compared with others)—**Para mí, el español es fácil.**

for (in the employ of)—**Trabajo para la universidad.**

Don't confuse the third person singular form of the verb *para* ("he/she stops," "you stop") with the preposition para. The context should tell you which part of speech and which meaning is most logical.

Some Uses of *Por*

Por is used to express the following:

by, by means of	**por tren, por avión, por teléfono**
through, along	**por la playa o por el parque**
during, in (time period)	**por la mañana, por la tarde**
because of, due to	**estoy nerviosa por el examen**
for, in exchange for	**Te doy $20 por el libro.**
for the sake of	**Lo hago por la familia.**
for, in order to get	**Voy por café.**
for (for a period of time)	**Estaré aquí por dos horas.**

In idiomatic expressions:

por Dios	for Heaven's sake	**por lo general**	in general
por ejemplo	for example	**por lo menos**	at least
por eso	that's why	**por si acaso**	just in case
por favor	please	**por primera/**	for the first/
por fin	finally	**última vez**	last time

EXPRESSIONS
"Yes / No" Questions

A common way to ask a yes/no question in Spanish is simply to change the intonation of your voice by making your voice rise at the end of the question: *¿Usted trabaja en México?* Another way to form a question is to invert the order of the subject and verb, in addition to making your voice rise at the end of the question: *¿Trabaja usted en México?; ¿Está todo bien?; ¿Necesita usted algo más?*

To answer a question affirmatively, begin with *Sí* ("yes"): *Sí, trabajo en México.* To answer a question negatively, begin with *No*, and place another no in front of the verb: *No, no trabajo en México.*

Notice that the word "do" from English ("Do you work?") is not translated into Spanish when asking a question.

Ways to Express Polite Requests

There are a number of ways to express polite requests in Spanish. For example, you can use a command, accompanied by *por favor* ("please"): *Tráigame un café, por favor.* A more polite way of making the same request, however, is to use a form of the verb querer: *¿Quiere traerme un café?;* (Literally: "do you want to bring me a coffee?").

You can also use the verb *querer* when you want to ask for a favor or make a polite inquiry: *Querría hacer una llamada a los Estados Unidos* ("I would like to make a phone call") OR *Quisiera hacer una llamada a los Estados Unidos* ("I would like to make a phone call").

Sometimes you can use the verb poder the same way: *¿Puede usted decirme?* ("Can you tell me?") OR *¿Podría usted indicarme?* ("Could you show me?").

Greetings and Polite Expressions

Buenos días.	Good morning, Good day.
Buenas tardes.	Good afternoon.
Buenas noches.	Good evening, Good night.
¡Hola!	Hi!
¿Cómo está usted?	How are you? (formal)
¿Cómo estás?	How are you? (informal)

¿Qué tal estás?	How are you? (informal)
¿Qué tal?	What's going on? How are things?
Muy bien, gracias.	Very well, thank you.
Adiós. Hasta luego.	Good-bye. Until later.
Hasta mañana.	Until tomorrow.
Muchas gracias.	Thanks very much.
De nada.	You're welcome.
Por favor.	Please.
Perdón. Con permiso.	Excuse me. Pardon me.

Introducing People

INFORMAL

Antonio, ¿conoces a mi amigo, Paco?
Antonio, do you know my friend, Paco?

Antonio, quiero presentarte a mi amigo, Paco.
Antonio, I'd like to introduce you to my friend, Paco.

Hola. ¿Qué tal?
Hi, how are you doing?

FORMAL

Sr. Rodríguez, permítame presentarle a mi socio, Santiago Silva
Mr. Rodríguez, allow me to introduce you to my partner, Santiago Silva.

Sra. Silva, le presento a la Sra. Rodríguez.
Mrs. Silva, I'd like you to meet Mrs. Rodríguez.

Mucho gusto.
It's a pleasure to meet you.

El gusto es mío.
The pleasure is mine.

TIME
Telling Time

To ask what time it is in Spanish, ask *¿Qué hora es?* To ask at what time something will happen, ask *¿A qué hora....?*

Use the verb *ser* to tell the time. "One o'clock" and any variation of one o'clock will use the singular form of the verb, *es*: *Es la una, es la una y diez, es la una y media*. With all numbers above one, use *son*: *Son las dos, son las nueve, son las once y veinte,* etc. Past the half hour, you should go to the next hour and subtract the minutes (3:50 = "It's ten to four" = *Son las cuatro menos diez*).

The word *media* means "half," and *cuarto* means "a quarter." *Son las cinco y media* (5:30), *son las nueve y cuarto* (9:15), *son las once menos cuarto* (10:45). Other useful expressions are *en punto* ("on the dot"), *de la mañana* ("a.m."), *de la tarde* ("p.m.") or *de la noche* ("p.m."), *la medianoche* ("midnight"), and *el mediodía* ("noon").

Days of the Week

Los días de la semana . . . .("the days of the week")
el lunes . . . . .Monday; on Monday
el martes . . . . .Tuesday; on Tuesday
el miércoles . . . . .Wednesday; on Wednesday
el jueves . . . . .Thursday; on Thursday
el viernes . . . . .Friday; on Friday
el sábado . . . . .Saturday; on Saturday
el domingo . . . . .Sunday; on Sunday

Notice that the days of the week in Spanish are not capitalized. When you want to indicate that something happens every Monday, every Saturday, etc., use the plural form of the article: *los lunes, los sábados,* etc.

Note: On the Hispanic calendar, the first day of the week is Monday. Other useful phrases: *mañana* ("tomorrow"), *pasado mañana* ("day after tomorrow"), *hoy* ("today"), *esta noche* ("tonight").

Dates, Seasons, Months of the Year

La fecha . . . . .The date
¿Cuál es la fecha de hoy? . . . . .What is today's date?
(Hoy) Es el primero de abril. . . . . .Today is April 1.
(Hoy) Es el cinco de marzo. . . . . .Today is March 5.

Note: The ordinal number primero is used to express the first day of the month, but cardinal numbers (*dos, tres,* etc.) are used for the other days.

Los meses del año ("the months of the year"):

enero . . . . .January		**febrero** . . . . .February
marzo . . . . . . .March		**abril** . . . . .April
mayo . . . . .May		**junio** . . . . .June
julio . . . . .July		**agosto** . . . . .August
septiembre . . . . .September		**octubre** . . . . .October
noviembre . . . .November		**diciembre** . . . . . . .December

Note: The months are not capitalized in Spanish.

Las estaciones del año ("the seasons of the year"):
el invierno . . . . .winter
la primavera . . .spring
el verano . . . . . .summer
el otoño . . . . . . .fall

Holidays and Special Occasions

la Semana Santa . . . . .Holy Week
la Pascua (Florida) . . . . .Easter
el Día de Independencia . . . . .Independence Day
el Día de los Muertos . . . . .All Soul's Day
la Nochebuena .Christmas Eve
la Navidad . . . . .Christmas
la Noche Vieja .New Year's Eve
el Día de Año Nuevo . . . . .New Year's Day
el aniversario . . . . .anniversary
el cumpleaños .birthday
los días festivos/las fiestas . . . . .holidays
las vacaciones .vacation
¡felicitaciones! .congratulations

NUMBERS
Numbers 1–100

1	uno	19	diecinueve
2	dos	20	veinte
3	tres	21	veintiuno
4	cuatro	22	veintidós
5	cinco	23	veintitrés
6	seis	24	veinticuatro, etc.
7	siete	30	treinta
8	ocho	31	treinta y uno
9	nueve	32	treinta y dos, etc.
10	diez	40	cuarenta
11	once	41	cuarenta y uno, etc.
12	doce	50	cincuenta
13	trece	60	sesenta
14	catorce	70	setenta
15	quince	80	ochenta
16	dieciséis	90	noventa
17	diecisiete	100	cien
18	dieciocho		

Numbers Above 100

101	ciento uno/una	700	setecientos/as
200	doscientos/as	800	ochocientos/as
300	trescientos/as	900	novecientos/as
400	cuatrocientos/as	1.000	mil
500	quinientos/as	2.000	dos mil
600	seiscientos/as	1.000.000	un millón

Ciento is used with numbers from 1–99 to express numbers 101–199: *ciento setenta y nueve,* etc. *Cien* is used in counting and before numbers greater than 999: *cien mil, cien millones,* etc. When numbers 200–900 precede a noun, they agree in gender: *trescientas habitaciones,* etc. In counting, *mil* does not have a plural form (*tres mil, seis mil*) but millón does: *dos millones, cinco millones,* etc.

Ordinal Numbers

primer(o) . . . . .first	**sexto** . . . . .sixth
segundo . . . . .second	**séptimo** . . . . .seventh
tercer(o) . . . . .third	**octavo** . . . . .eighth
cuarto . . . . .fourth	**noveno** . . . . .ninth
quinto . . . . .fifth	**décimo** . . . . .tenth

Ordinal numbers are adjectives and must agree with the noun they describe: *la octava semana, el sexto piso, el cuarto día, la primera semana,* etc. Notice that *primero* and *tercero* drop off the *-o* when they precede a masculine noun: *el primer día, el tercer día.*

Generally speaking, ordinal numbers above ten are not commonly used in Spanish. You will hear native speakers say instead, *el piso (número) veinte, la lección (número) catorce* and so forth.

LEARN TO SPEAK SPANISH

Vocabulary

Spanish	English	Spanish	English
a continuación	further on	*la actriz*	actress
a la derecha	to, on the right	*acumulado*	accumulated
a la derecha de	to the right of	*adiós*	good-bye
a la izquierda	to, on the left	*¿adónde?*	where? to where?
a la izquierda de	to the left of	*el aeropuerto*	airport
a la vuelta	around the corner	*afeitarse*	to shave
a partir de	starting on	*las afueras*	suburbs, outskirts
¿a qué hora?	what time? at what time?	*la agencia de viajes*	travel agency
a veces	sometimes	*el agente*	agent
abierto	open	*agosto*	August
el abogado	lawyer	*agradable*	pleasant
abrazar	to embrace	*agrio*	sour
abril	April	*el agua*	water
abrir	to open	*el agua mineral*	mineral water
la abuela	grandmother	*el aguacate*	avocado
el abuelo	grandfather	*agudo*	sharp
el aburrimiento	boredom	*ahí*	there
el aceite	oil	*ahora*	now
aceptar	accept	*ahora mismo*	right away
acompañar	to go with, accompany	*los ahorros*	savings
el acondicionador	conditioner	*el aire*	air
aconsejar	to advise	*el ajo*	garlic
acostarse	to go to bed	*al*	to the
acostumbrado	to be used to	*al final*	at the end
		al lado de	next to, beside
el actor	actor	*alcohólico*	alcoholic

97

alegrarse	to be glad	*apetecer*	to appeal to
algo	something	*el apio*	celery
alguien	someone	*aplaudir*	to applaud
algún	some, any	*aquel*	that (over there)
allá	there	*aquellos*	those (over there)
el almidón	starch	*aquí*	here
la almohada	pillow	*aquí tiene*	here you are
el almuerzo	lunch	*la araña*	spider
el alojamiento	hotel accomodations	*el arquitecto*	architect
el altar	altar	*arreglar*	to fix
la altitud	altitude	*arriba*	above
amable	kind	*el arroyo*	creek
amarillo	yellow	*el arroyo*	creek
la ambulancia	ambulance	*el arroz*	rice
amueblado	furnished	*el ascensor*	elevator
anaranjado	orange	*así*	so that, that way
andar	to walk	*el asiento*	seat
el andén	platform	*asistir a*	to attend
angosto	narrow	*la aspiradora*	vacuum cleaner
animado	lively	*el asteroide*	asteroid
el aniversario	anniversary	*atrás*	in the back
el año	year	*el atún*	tuna
anoche	last night	*el autobús*	bus
antes	sooner, before	*el automóvil*	car
antes de	before	*la avenida*	avenue
anunciar	to announce	*el avión*	airplane
el aparato	machine	*ayudar*	to help
el apartamento	apartment	*el azúcar*	sugar
		azul	blue

bailar	to dance	*el botón*	button
el balance	balance (account balance)	*el botones*	bellhop
		el bou	type of fishing boat
el balcón	balcony	*el brazo*	arm
la banana	banana	*el brócili*	broccoli
bañarse	to take a bath	*bucear*	to scuba dive
el baño	bathroom	*buenas noches*	good night
barato	cheap, inexpensive	*buenas tardes*	good afternoon/evening
la barbilla	chin		
la barca	ferry	*bueno*	good
el barco	ship	*Bueno.*	O.K., Fine.
barrer	to sweep	*¿beuno?*	hello?
bastante	rather, enough	*buenos días*	good morning
el baúl	trunk	*el bulevar*	boulevard
el bebé	baby	*buscar*	to look for
beber	to drink	*el caballo*	horse
la bebida	drink, beverage	*la cabeza*	head
la bicicleta	bicycle	*cada*	each
bien	well, fine	*la cadera*	hip
el billete	bill (paper money)	*el café*	coffee
el bistec	steak	*el caimán*	alligator
blanco	white	*la caja*	cash register
la blusa	blouse	*el cajero*	cashier
la bocina	horn	*los calcetines*	socks
el boleto	ticket	*la calculadora*	calculator
la bolsa	bag	*la calle*	street
la bomba	gasoline pump	*los calzoncillos*	men's underwear
el bosque	forest	*la cama*	bed
la bota	boot	*la cama*	double bed

LEARN TO SPEAK SPANISH

el camarero	waiter	catorce	fourteen
los camarones	shrimp	caurenta y ocho	forty-eight
cambiar	to change	la causa	cause
el cambio	exchange rate	la cena	dinner
caminar	to walk	el cenicero	ashtray
la camisa	shirt	el centro	downtown
la camiseta	undershirt, t-shirt	el cepillo	brush
la campiña	countryside	cerca de	near, close to
el campo	country, countryside	cero	zero
		cerrar	to close
la canción	song	la cerveza	beer
el cantante	singer	el chaleco	vest
la cantidad	quantity	el champú	shampoo
cargar a la habitación	to charge to the room	la chaqueta	jacket
		la chaqueta	jacket
la carne	meat	el cheque	check
la carne asada	roast beef	el cheque de viaje	traveler's check
la carne de cerdo	pork	el cheque de viajero	traveler's check
la carne de res	beef		
la carnicería	meat counter, butcher shop	chillón	loud (e.g. colors)
		el chocolate	chocolate
el carnicero	butcher	la chuleta de cerdo	pork chop
caro	expensive	cien	one hundred
la carretera	highway	cinco	five
el carro	car	cincuenta	fifty
la carta	letter	cincuenta y cinco	fifty-five
la casa	house	cincuenta y cuatro	fifty-four
casado	married	cincuenta y dos	fifty-two
la cascada	waterfall	cincuenta y nueve	fifty-nine
casi	almost		

cincuenta y ocho	fifty-eight	*comprar*	to buy
cincuenta y seis	fifty-six	*comprender*	to understand
cincuenta y siete	fifty-seven	*la computadora*	computer
cincuenta y tres	fifty-three	*con*	with
cincuenta y uno	fifty-one	*con antelación*	in advance
el cine	movie theater	*conocer*	to know, meet
el cinturón	belt	*conseguir*	to get, acquire
la ciudad	city	*el consomé de pollo*	chicken soup
claro	of course		
la clase	class	*construir*	to build
clásico	classic	*consultar*	to consult
la cobija	blanket	*contestar*	to answer
cobrar	to cash	*contigo*	with you
el coche	car	*continuo*	continuous
la cocina	kitchen	*convenir*	to be convenient
el cocinero	cook, chef	*conversar*	to talk with, converse
el coco	coconut		
el cocodrilo	crocodile	*la corbata*	tie
el codo	elbow	*cortarse el pelo*	to cut one's hair
el cofre	hood	*coser*	to sew
coincidir	to coincide	*la costa*	coast
la coliflor	cauliflower	*costar*	to cost
colonial	colonial	*el coulomb*	coulomb (Physics)
el color	color	*creer*	to believe
el comedor	dining room	*el cuaderno*	notebook
comer	to eat	*la cuadra*	block
la comida	food	*el cuadro*	painting
¿cómo?	how?	*¿cuándo?*	when?
¡Cómo no!	Of course!	*¿cuánto?*	how much?
		¿cuántos?	how many?

101

LEARN TO SPEAK SPANISH

cuarenta	forty	*de nada*	you're welcome
cuarenta y cinco	forty-five	*de paso*	while you're at it
cuarenta y cuatro	forty-four	*de persona a persona*	person to person
cuarenta y dos	forty-two		
cuarenta y nueve	forty-nine	*de ser posible*	if it's possible
cuarenta y seis	forty-six	*de vacaciones*	on vacation
cuarenta y siete	forty-seven	*debajo de*	under
cuarenta y tres	forty-three	*deber*	to be ought to, should, must
cuarenta y uno	forty-one		
cuarto	fourth	*débil*	weak
el cuarto de baño	bathroom	*décimo*	tenth
cuatro	four	*decir*	to tell
cuatrocientos	four hundred	*dejar*	to leave, let
el cubo	cube	*del*	of the, about the
la cuenta	bill, check, account	*delante de*	in front of
la cuenta corriente	checking account	*delicioso*	delicious
la cuenta de ahorros	savings account	*demasiado*	too much
		la demora	delay
el cuidado	care	*dentro de*	within
cuidarse	to take care of oneself	*depender de*	to depend on
		la dependienta	salesclerk
el cumpleaños	birthday	*depositar*	to deposit
la cuñada	sister-in-law	*el depósito*	deposit
la cuota	quota	*el desayuno*	breakfast
dar	to give	*descansar*	to rest
dar clases	to give classes, teach	*desde hace*	since, it's been
		desear	to want
de	of	*desinflado*	flat, not inflated
de acuerdo	O.K., in agreement	*despertarse*	to wake up
de cuero	leather	*después*	after, afterwards

después de	after	*diurno*	daily
detrás de	behind	*divertirse*	to enjoy oneself
la deuda	debt	*dividir*	to divide
el día	day	*divorciado*	divorced
el Día de Año Nuevo	New Year's Day	*doblar*	to turn
		doce	twelve
el Día de Independencia	Independence Day	*el doctor*	doctor
		documentar	to check, document (the luggage)
el Día de los Muertos	All Soul's Day		
		el dólar	dollar
diario	daily	*doler*	to hurt
la diarrea	diarrhea	*el dolor*	pain
diciembre	December	*el dolor de estómago*	stomach ache
diecinueve	nineteen		
dieciocho	eighteen	*el domingo*	Sunday
dieciséis	sixteen	*¿dónde?*	where?
diecisiete	seventeen	*dormirse*	to fall asleep
diez	ten	*el dormitorio*	bedroom
difícil	difficult	*dos*	two
¿dígame?	May I help you?	*doscientos*	two hundred
el dinero	money	*doscientos*	two hundred
la dirección	address	*dulce*	sweet
directamente	directly	*duodécimo*	twelfth
directo	direct	*durante*	during
la directora	director	*economizar*	to budget, save
el disco	record	*el ecuador*	equator
discreto	discreet, subtle	*el efectivo*	cash
disfrutar	to enjoy	*el efecto*	effect
disímil	dissimilar	*él*	he
el distribuidor	distributor	*la electricidad*	electricity

LEARN TO SPEAK SPANISH

elegante	elegant	*entre*	between
el elenco	cast	*envolver*	to wrap up
ella	she, her	*el equipaje*	luggage
ellos	they, them	*equivocarse*	to make a mistake, be mistaken
el embarque	boarding		
el embotellamiento	traffic jam	*las escaleras*	stairs
empezar	to begin	*el escenario*	stage
el empleado	employee	*la escoba*	broom
el empleado de servicio	attendant	*escribir*	to write
		la escuela	school
en efectivo	in cash	*ese*	that (that one)
en efecto	that's correct, right	*ese*	that (nearby)
en frente de	in front of	*esos*	those (nearby)
en la esquina	at, on the corner	*el espacio*	space
en tournée	on tour	*especial*	special
encantado	pleased, happy (to meet you)	*la especialidad*	specialty, special
		el espejo	mirror
encantar	to love, please	*esperar*	to wait, hope
encargar	to request	*la esposa*	wife
el encargo	order, job	*el esposo*	husband
las enchiladas suizas	chicken enchiladas	*la esquina*	corner
		está bien	alright
encima de	on top of	*la estación de tren*	train station
encontrar	to find	*los Estados Unidos*	the United States
enero	January	*estar*	to be
el enfermero	nurse	*estar de visita*	to be visiting
la ensalada verde	green salad	*estar de vuelta*	to be back
enseñar	to show	*este*	this
entonces	then, so	*éste*	this one
la entrada	ticket		

estos	these	*el fregasuelos*	mop
estrenar	to debut	*los frenos*	brakes
el estudiante	student	*la frente*	forehead
la estufa	stove	*frente a*	facing
estupendo	fantastic, great	*la fresa*	strawberry
el eufemismo	euphemism	*fresco*	fresh
la Europa	Europe	*frío*	cold
evitar	to avoid	*la fruta*	fruit
la excursión	trip, tour	*el frutero*	fruit vendor
el excursionismo a pie	hiking	*la fuente*	fountain
		fuera de	outside
extraño	strange	*fumar*	to smoke
el faisán	pheasant	*la función*	show
la falda	skirt	*funcionar*	to work, function
la familia	family	*el garaje*	garage
los faros	headlights	*los gemelos*	twins
febrero	February	*gracias*	thank you
la felicidad	happiness	*grande*	large, big
¡felicitaciones!	congratulations	*la grasa*	grease, fat
la ferretería	hardware store	*gris*	gray
la fiesta	party	*la grúa*	tow truck
el final	end	*el guante*	glove
el flan	custard	*el gusano*	worm
el flequillo	bangs	*gustar*	to be pleasing to, to like
folklórico	folkloric		
los fondos	funds	*el gusto*	taste
las frambuesas	raspberries	*la habitación*	room
frecuente	frequent	*hablar*	to speak, talk
el fregadero	sink	*habrá*	there will, it will

LEARN TO SPEAK SPANISH

hace buen tiempo	it's nice weather	*los hijos*	children, sons
hace calor	it's hot	*la hilera*	row
hace fresco	it's cool	*la historia*	history
hace frío	it's cold	*hola*	hello, hi
hace mal tiempo	it's bad weather	*el hombre*	man
hace sol	it's sunny	*la hora*	hour
hace viento	it's windy	*el horno*	oven
hacer	to make, do	*horroroso*	horrible, horrifying
hacer camping	to camp	*el hotel*	hotel
hacer juego con	to match with	*hoy*	today
hacer la cama	to make the bed	*hoy*	today
hacer las compras	to do the shopping	*el huevo*	egg
hacer un viaje	to take a trip	*igualmente*	equally
hacer una llamada	to make a call	*incluir*	to include
hacerse una permanente	to get a permanent	*la industria*	industry, manufacturing company
la hamaca	hammock	*la información*	information
la hamburguesa	hamburger	*el ingeniero*	engineer
la harina	flour	*la inmobiliaria*	rental agency
hasta	until	*insistir*	to insist, keep trying
hasta allá	to that place, there	*la intención*	
hasta luego	until then, see you later		intention
hay	there is, there are	*el interés*	interest
el helado	ice cream	*interesante*	interesting
el helicóptero	helicopter	*invertir*	to invest
la hermana	sister	*el invierno*	Winter
el hermano	brother	*el invitado*	guest
el hielo	ice	*invitar*	to invite

ir a	to go to, be going to	*lavar en seco*	to dryclean
ir de vacaciones	to go on vacation	*lavarse*	to wash oneself
el jabón	soap	*lavarse el pelo*	to wash one's hair
el jamón	ham	*le*	to him, to her, to you (formal)
el jefe	chief	*la leche*	milk
la jirafa	giraffe	*lejos*	far
el joule	joule (Physics)	*lejos de*	far, far from
el jueves	Thursday	*la lengua*	tongue
jugar	to play	*lento*	slow
el jugo	juice	*el león*	lion
el juguete	toy	*les*	to them, to you (plural, formal)
julio	July	*levantarse*	to get up
junio	June	*las libras*	pounds
junto a	next to	*libre*	free, available
justo	exactly, just	*la librería*	bookstore
ka	letter k	*el libro*	book
el karate	karate	*el limón*	lime, lemon
el kilo	kilogram, kilo	*la limonada*	limonade
el kinesiólogo	kinesiologist	*limpiar*	to clean
kurdo	Kurdish	*lindo*	pretty
el labio	lip	*liso*	smooth
el laboratorio	laboratory	*listo*	ready
la lana	wool	*la llamada*	call, phone call
la langosta	lobster	*llamar*	to call
la lavadora	washing machine	*llamar en la puerta*	to knock on the door
la lavandería	laundry	*llamarse*	to be named, called
el lavaplatos	dishwasher	*la llanta*	tire
lavar	to wash		

LEARN TO SPEAK SPANISH

llegar	to arrive	*marcar*	to dial
llenar	to fill	*marcharse*	to leave, go away
llevar	to take, carry	*el marido*	husband
llevar mucho tiempo	to take a long time	*los mariscos*	seafood
		marrón	brown
la lluvia	rain	*el martes*	Tuesday
lo	it	*marzo*	March
lo	him, you (formal)	*más*	more
lo siento	I'm sorry	*más bien*	more like
el lobo	wolf	*más tarde*	later
los	them, you (plural, formal)	*el matrimonio*	married couple
		mayo	May
Luis	Louis	*mayor*	older
el lunes	Monday	*me*	to me
la madre	mother	*me*	to me
el maestro	teacher	*la medicina*	medicine
mal	badly, ill	*el médico*	doctor
el malestar general	general feeling of illness	*medio*	half
		las mejillas	cheeks
la maleta	suitcase	*mejor*	better
malhumorado	in a bad mood	*mejor*	better
la mamá	mom, mother	*mejorarse*	to get better
mañana	tomorrow	*el melon*	melon
mandar un fax	to send a fax	*menor*	younger
manejar	to drive	*menos*	less
el mango	mango	*el mercado*	market
el mantel	tablecloth	*la merienda*	snack
la mantequilla	butter	*la mermelada*	jam
la manzana	apple	*meter*	to put in
el mar	sea		

el metro	subway	*el negativo*	negative
mexicano	Mexican	*negro*	black
México	Mexico	*ni*	neither, nor
mi	my	*la niebla*	fog
el microondas	microwave	*el nieto*	grandchild
el microscopio	microscope	*ningún*	no, none
el miércoles	Wednesday	*los niños*	children
mil	one thousand	*no hay de que*	it's nothing, you're welcome
mirar	to look, look at	*no tener razón*	to be wrong
el momento	moment	*la noche*	night
la montaña	mountain	*la Noche Vieja*	New Year's Eve
los monumentos	historic sites	*la Nochebuena*	Christmas Eve
morado	purple	*el nombre*	name
la motocicleta	motorcycle	*normalmente*	normally
el motor	engine	*norteamericano*	North American, from the U.S.
mucho	a lot, much		
los muebles	furniture	*nos*	to us
la mujer	woman, wife	*nosotros*	we, us
la música	music	*novecientos*	nine hundred
el músico	musician	*noveno*	ninth
muy	very	*noventa*	ninety
Muy amable.	You're very kind.	*noventa (90)*	ninety
nada	nothing	*noventa y cinco*	ninety-five
nadar	to swim	*noventa y cuatro*	ninety-four
nadie	no one	*noventa y dos*	ninety-two
la naranja	orange (fruit)	*noventa y nueve*	ninety-nine
la nariz	nose	*noventa y ocho*	ninety-eight
la Navidad	Christmas	*noventa y seis*	ninety-six
necesitar	to need		

LEARN TO SPEAK SPANISH

noventa y siete	ninety-seven
noventa y tres	ninety-three
noventa y uno	ninety-one
noviembre	November
la nube	cloud
las nueces	nuts
las nueve	nine o'clock
nueve	nine
nuevo	new
el número	number
nunca	never
o	either, or
la ocasión	occasion
ochenta	eighty
ochenta y cinco	eighty-five
ochenta y cuatro	eighty-four
ochenta y dos	eighty-two
ochenta y nueve	eighty-nine
ochenta y ocho	eighty-eight
ochenta y seis	eighty-six
ochenta y siete	eighty-seven
ochenta y tres	eighty-three
ochenta y uno	eighty-one
ocho	eight
ochocientos	eight hundred
octavo	eighth
octubre	October
ocurrir	to occur
la oficina	office
la oficina de cambio	exchange office
la oficina de correos	post office
la oficina de información	information office
ofrecer	to offer
el ojo	eye
la olla	pot
olvidarse de	to forget about
once	eleven
la operadora	operator
os	to you (plural, informal)
el oso	bear
el otoño	Autumn
otro	other
el padre	father
los padres	parents
pagar	to pay
la página	page
el país	country, nation
el pan	bread
la pantalla	screen
el pantalón	pants
los pantalones	pants
el pañuelo	scarf
las papas fritas	fried potatoes, french fries
el par	pair
para	for

el parabrisas	windshield		*la peluquería*	beauty shop
parecer	to seem		*pensar*	to think
el parque nacional	national park		*pensar en*	to think about
la parte	part		*peor*	worse
el pasaje	ticket, airline ticket		*pequeño*	small
el pasajero	passenger		*pequeño*	small
el pasaporte	passport		*perderse*	to get lost
pasar	to come in, pass		*perdón*	excuse me
pasar la aspiradora	to run the vacuum cleaner		*perdone*	excuse me
			pero	but
pasar por	to go through		*la persona*	person
pasar unos días	to spend a few days		*pesado*	heavy
la Pascua (Florida)	Easter		*pesar*	to weigh
pasear	to stroll, walk		*el pescado*	fish
el pasillo	hallway		*el peso*	peso
la pasta	pasta		*la piel*	skin
la pastilla	pill		*la pierna*	leg
el patio	patio		*el piloto*	pilot
pedir	to order, ask for		*la pimienta*	pepper
peinarse	to comb		*la piña*	pineapple
el peine	comb		*el piso*	floor, story of a building
la película	movie			
el pelo	hair		*la pista*	runway
el pelo lacio	straight hair		*planchar*	to iron
el pelo ondulado	wavy hair		*el plástico*	plastic
el pelo rizado	curly hair		*plateado*	silver
la pelota	ball		*la playa*	beach
la peluca	wig		*la plaza de garaje*	garage space
la peluquera	hair dresser		*las plazas*	seats, spaces

LEARN TO SPEAK SPANISH

poder	to be able, can
el policía	police officer
el pollo	chicken
el polvo	dust
el poncho	poncho
poner	to put
ponerse	to put on
ponerse moreno	to get tanned
por	per, for
por cierto	by the way, incidentally
por cobrar	collect, reversing the charges
por Dios	for Heaven's sake
por ejemplo	for example
por eso	that's why
por favor	please
por fin	finally
por lo general	in general
por lo menos	at least
por si acaso	just in case
por supuesto	of course
porque	because
posible	possible
el postre	dessert
el precio	price
preciso	necessary
preferir	to prefer
preguntar	to ask

preocuparse	to worry
la primavera	Spring
primero	first
el primo	cousin
privado	private
el producto	product
el profesor	professor
pronto	soon
próximo	next
el pueblo	town, village
el puente	bridge
la puerta	door, gate
el puerto	port
pues	well
el pulgar	thumb
las puntas	ends of hair
que	that, which
¿qué?	what?
quedar	to stay, remain, be
quedarle bien	to look good on one
quedarse	to stay
quedarse calvo	to go bald
Quédese con la vuelta.	Keep the change.
quemar	to burn
querer	to want
el queso	cheese
¿quién?	who? whom?

quince	fifteen	reservado	reserved
quince	fifteen	reservar	to reserve
quinientos	five hundred	el restaurante	restaurant
quinto	fifth	la reunión	meeting
quitar	to remove	revisar	to check
quitarse	to take off	el rey	king
Quito	Quito	rico	rich, delicious
quizás	maybe	los rizos	curls
la rana	frog	rojo	red
el rayo	lightening	la ropa	clothes
rebelde	rebellious	la ropa interior	underwear
el recado	message	la rueda	wheel
el recepcionista	receptionist	el ruedo	hem
la receta	prescription	el ruido	noise
recibir	to receive	el sábado	Saturday
recibir una llamada	to receive a call	la sábana	sheet (bed sheet)
		saber	to know
recoger	to pick up	sacar	to withdraw
recomendar	to recommend	la sal	salt
recorrer	to travel along	la sala	living room
el refresco	softdrink	la sala de espera	waiting room
el refrigerador	refrigerator	la sala de estar	living room
regresar	to return	la salchicha	sausage
la reina	queen	la salida	departure, exit
el remiendo	patch	salir	to leave
la representación	show	la sandalia	sandal
la representación de teatro	play (drama)	la sandía	watermelon
		el sauce	willow
la reservación	reservation	la secadora	dryer

LEARN TO SPEAK SPANISH

la secadora de pelo	hairdryer	*ser*	to be
secar	to dry	*la serpiente*	snake
la sección	section	*sesenta*	sixty
la sección de no fumar	non-smoking section	*sesenta y cinco*	sixty-five
		sesenta y cuatro	sixty-four
seco	dry (adj.)	*sesenta y dos*	sixty-two
la secretaria	secretary	*sesenta y nueve*	sixty-nine
la seda	silk	*sesenta y ocho*	sixty-eight
seguir	to follow, continue	*sesenta y seis*	sixty-six
segundo	second	*sesenta y siete*	sixty-seven
seguro	sure	*sesenta y tres*	sixty-three
seis	six	*sesenta y uno*	sixty-one
seiscientos	six hundred	*setecientos*	seven hundred
la selección	selection	*setenta*	seventy
el semáforo	traffic light	*setenta y cinco*	seventy-five
la semana	week	*setenta y cuatro*	seventy-four
la semana libre	week off	*setenta y dos*	seventy-two
la Semana Santa	Easter week	*setenta y nueve*	seventy-nine
la señal de alto	stop sign	*setenta y ocho*	seventy-eight
el señor	man, sir, Mr.	*setenta y seis*	seventy-six
la señora	woman, ma'am, Mrs.	*setenta y siete*	seventy-seven
		setenta y tres	seventy-three
sentarse	to sit down	*setenta y uno*	seventy-one
sentarse	to sit down, seat oneself	*sexto*	sixth
		si	if
sentir	to feel	*sí*	yes
sentirse	to feel	*siempre*	always
sentirse	to feel	*la sierra*	saw
septiembre	September	*siete*	seven
séptimo	seventh		

siguiente	next		*tardar*	to take time
sin	without		*tarde*	late
sobre	about		*la tarde*	afternoon
el sobre	envelope		*la tarjeta de crédito*	credit card
sobre todo	above all		*la tarjeta telefónica*	phone card
el sobrino	nephew		*el taxi*	taxi
el socio	colleague, partner		*el taxista*	taxi driver
el sol	sun		*la taza*	cup
solo	just, alone		*la taza*	cup
sólo	only, just		*el tazón*	bowl
soltero	single		*te*	to you (informal)
el sombrero	hat		*el té*	tea
el sostén	bra		*el teatro*	theater
su	your (formal)		*el techo*	roof
subir	to go up, get on		*el técnico*	repairman
sucio	dirty		*el teléfono*	telephone
el sucre	sucre		*el telegrama*	telegram
suelto	loose		*la televisión*	television
el suéter	sweater		*el televisor*	television
el supermercado	supermarket		*el tema*	subject, topic
el sur	south		*las tenazas*	curling iron
la talla	size		*tener*	to have
también	also		*tener calor*	to be hot
tampoco	neither		*tener cuidado*	to be careful
el tanque	tank		*tener fiebre*	to have a fever
tanto	so much, as much		*tener frío*	to be cold
tantos	so many		*tener ganas de*	to feel like
el tapón de rueda	hubcap		*tener ganas de*	to feel like (doing something)
la taquilla	ticket booth			

LEARN TO SPEAK SPANISH

tener hambre	to be hungry	*la toronja*	grapefruit
tener miedo	to be afraid	*la torta de chocolate*	chocolate cake
tener náuseas	to be nauseous		
tener prisa	to be in a hurry	*el tour*	tour
tener que	to have to (do something)	*el tour organizado*	organized tour
		trabajar	to work
tener que	to have to	*el trabajo*	work
tener razón	to be right	*traer*	to bring
tener sed	to be thirsty	*el tráfico*	traffic
tener sueño	to be sleepy	*el traje*	suit
tener... años	to be years old	*la transferencia*	transfer
tercero	third	*tratar*	to try
terminar	to finish, end	*tratar de*	to try to
la ternera	veal	*trece*	thirteen
terrible	terrible	*treinta (30)*	thirty
el tiempo	time, weather	*treinta y cinco*	thirty-five
el tiempo libre	free time	*treinta y cuatro*	thirty-four
la tienda	store	*treinta y dos*	thirty-two
las tijeras	scissors	*treinta y nueve*	thirty-nine
la tintorería	dry cleaner's	*treinta y ocho*	thirty-eight
el tío	uncle	*treinta y seis*	thirty-six
la toalla	towel	*treinta y siete*	thirty-seven
todavía	still, yet	*treinta y tres*	thirty-three
todavía no	not yet	*treinta y uno*	thirty-one
todo derecho	straight ahead	*el tren*	train
todos	all	*tres (3)*	three
tomar	to take, drink, eat	*trescientos*	three hundred
tomar una copa	to have a drink	*trescientos*	three hundred
la tormenta	storm	*triunfar*	to triumph

el triunfo	victory	*veintiuno*	twenty-one
tú	you (informal)	*venir*	to come
los tubos eléctricos	electric curlers	*venirle bien*	to suit one
último	last	*la ventaja*	advantage
un	a	*la ventana*	window
un par de	a pair of, a couple of	*ver*	to see
un poco	a little	*el verano*	Summer
la uña	fingernail	*¿verdad?*	right?
la universidad	university	*la verdad*	truth
uno	one	*verde*	green
unos	some	*la verdura*	vegetable
usted	you (formal)	*las verduras*	vegetables
ustedes	you (formal, plural)	*verse*	to see one another
la uva	grape	*el vértigo*	dizziness
las uvas	grapes	*el vestido*	dress
la vaca	cow	*vestirse*	to get dressed
varios	several	*el viaje*	trip
el vaso	drinking glass	*viejo*	old
veinte	twenty	*el viento*	wind
veinte	twenty	*el viernes*	Friday
veinticinco	twenty-five	*el vino*	wine
veinticuatro	twenty-four	*la violeta*	violet
veintidos	twenty-two	*la viuda*	widow
veintinueve	twenty-nine	*la vivienda*	place to live, dwelling
veintiocho	twenty-eight	*vivir*	to live
veintiséis	twenty-six	*el volante*	steering wheel
veintisiete	twenty-seven	*el volumen*	volume
veintitrés	twenty-three	*volver a*	to return to, do again

LEARN TO SPEAK SPANISH

volver a llamar	call again	*yo*	I
vosotros	you (informal, plural)	*Yucatán*	Yucatan
el vuelo	flight	*las zanahorias*	carrots
el wafle	waffle	*el zapato*	shoe
Washington	Washington	*el zoológico*	zoo
el whisky	whiskey	*el zorro*	fox
Wilma	Wilma		
Wyoming	Wyoming		
Xavier	Xavier		
y	and		
ya	already		
la yegua	mare		

Note: This glossary is a reference of the vocabulary words introduced in the *Learn To Speak Spanish* program along with their English translations. It is not intended to be a comprehensive lexicon of the Spanish language.

Appendices
APPENDIX A: VERB REVIEW

I. REGULAR -AR VERBS: HABLAR (to speak)

Infinitive:	**hablar**	Imperative:	**habla (tú); no hables (tú)**
Gerund:	**hablando**		**hable (usted)**
Past Participle:	**hablado**		

	Present Indicative	Present Subjunctive	Preterite	Imperfect	Future	Conditional
yo	habl *o*	habl *e*	habl *é*	habl *aba*	hablar *é*	hablar *ía*
tú	habl *as*	habl *es*	habl *aste*	habl *abas*	hablar *ás*	hablar *ías*
él, ella, usted	habl *a*	habl *e*	habl *ó*	habl *aba*	hablar *á*	hablar *ía*
nosotros, nosotras	habl *amos*	habl *emos*	habl *amos*	habl *ábamos*	hablar *emos*	hablar *íamos*
vosotros, vosotras	habl *áis*	habl *éis*	habl *asteis*	habl *abais*	hablar *éis*	hablar *íais*
ellos, ellas, ustedes	habl *an*	habl *en*	habl *aron*	habl *aban*	hablar *án*	hablar *ían*

*The **Present Perfect** is conjugated with the auxiliary verb "*haber*" and the past participle: *he amado, has amado, ha amado, hemos amado, habéis amado, han amado.*

II. REGULAR -ER VERBS: *COMER* (to eat)

Infinitive: **comer**   Imperative: **come (tú); no comas (tú)**
Gerund: **comiendo**   **coma (usted)**
Past Participle: **comido**

	Present Indicative	Present Subjunctive	Preterite	Imperfect	Future	Conditional
yo	com *o*	com *a*	com *í*	com *ía*	comer *é*	comer *ía*
tú	com *es*	com *as*	com *iste*	com *ías*	comer *ás*	comer *ías*
él, ella, usted	com *e*	com *a*	com *ió*	com *ía*	comer *á*	comer *ía*
nosotros, nosotras	com *emos*	com *amos*	com *imos*	com *íamos*	comer *emos*	comer *íamos*
vosotros, vosotras	com *éis*	com *áis*	com *isteis*	com *íais*	comer *éis*	comer *íais*
ellos, ellas, ustedes	com *en*	com *an*	com *ieron*	com *ían*	comer *án*	comer *ían*

*The **Present Perfect** is conjugated with the auxiliary verb "*haber*" and the past participle: *he comido, has comido, ha comido, hemos comido, habéis comido, han comido.*

III. REGULAR *-IR* VERBS: *VIVIR* (to live)

Infinitive: **vivir** Imperative: **vive (tú); no vivas (tú)**
Gerund: **viviendo** **viva (usted)**
Past Participle: **vivido**

	Present Indicative	Present Subjunctive	Preterite	Imperfect	Future	Conditional
yo	viv *o*	viv *a*	viv *í*	viv *ía*	vivir *é*	vivir *ía*
tú	viv *es*	viv *as*	viv *iste*	viv *ías*	vivir *ás*	vivir *ías*
él, ella, usted	viv *e*	viv *a*	viv *ió*	viv *ía*	vivir *á*	vivir *ía*
nosotros, nosotras	viv *imos*	viv *amos*	viv *imos*	viv *íamos*	vivir *emos*	vivir *íamos*
vosotros, vosotras	viv *is*	viv *áis*	viv *isteis*	viv *íais*	vivir *éis*	vivir *íais*
ellos, ellas, ustedes	viv *en*	viv *an*	viv *ieron*	viv *ían*	vivir *án*	vivir *ían*

*The **Present Perfect** is conjugated with the auxiliary verb "*haber*" and the past participle: *he vivido, has vivido, ha vivido, hemos vivido, habéis vivido, han vivido.*

IV. SOME COMMONLY USED IRREGULAR VERBS

A. Dar (to give)

Infinitive: **dar**   Gerund: **dando**   Past Participle: **dado**

Imperative: **da (tú); no des (tú); dé (usted)**

	Present Indicative	Present Subjunctive	Preterite	Imperfect	Future	Conditional
yo	doy	dé	di	daba	daré	daría
tú	das	des	diste	dabas	darás	darías
él, ella, usted	da	dé	dio	daba	dará	daría
nosotros, nosotras	damos	demos	dimos	dábamos	daremos	daríamos
vosotros, vosotras	dais	deis	disteis	dabais	daréis	daríais
ellos, ellas, ustedes	dan	den	dieron	daban	darán	darían

B. *Decir* (to say)

Infinitive: **decir**   Gerund: **diciendo**   Past Participle: **dicho**

Imperative: **di (tú); no digas (tú); digaø (usted)**

	Present Indicative	Present Subjunctive	Preterite	Imperfect	Future	Conditional
yo	digo	diga	dije	decía	diré	diría
tú	dices	digas	dijiste	decías	dirás	dirías
él, ella, usted	dice	diga	dijo	decía	dirá	diría
nosotros, nosotras	decimos	digamos	dijimos	decíamos	diremos	diríamos
vosotros, vosotras	decís	digáis	dijisteis	decíais	diréis	diríais
ellos, ellas, ustedes	dicen	digan	dijeron	decían	dirán	dirían

C. *Estar* (to be)

Infinitive: **estar**　　　　Gerund: **estando**　　　Past Participle: **estado**
Imperative: **está (tú); no estés (tú); esté (usted)**

	Present Indicative	Present Subjunctive	Preterite	Imperfect	Future	Conditional
yo	estoy	esté	estuve	estaba	estaré	estaría
tú	estás	estés	estuviste	estabas	estarás	estarías
él, ella, usted	está	esté	estuvo	estaba	estará	estaría
nosotros, nosotras	estamos	estemos	estuvimos	estábamos	estaremos	estaríamos
vosotros, vosotras	estáis	estéis	estuvisteis	estabais	estaréis	estaríais
ellos, ellas, ustedes	están	estén	estuvieron	estaban	estarán	estarían

D. *Hacer* (to make; to do)

Infinitive: **hacer**　　　　Gerund: **haciendo**　　　Past Participle: **hecho**
Imperative: **haz (tú); no hagas (tú); haga (usted)**

	Present Indicative	Present Subjunctive	Preterite	Imperfect	Future	Conditional
yo	hago	haga	hice	hacía	haré	haría
tú	haces	hagas	hiciste	hacías	haras	harías
él, ella, usted	hace	haga	hizo	hacía	hará	haría
nosotros, nosotras	hacemos	hagamos	hicimos	hacíamos	haremos	haríamos
vosotros, vosotras	hacéis	hagáis	hicisteis	hacíais	haréis	haríais
ellos, ellas, ustedes	hacen	hagan	hicieron	hacían	harán	harían

E. *Ir* (to go)

Infinitive: **ir**   Gerund: **yendo**   Past Participle: **ido**
Imperative: **vé (tú); no vayas (tú); vaya (usted)**

	Present Indicative	Present Subjunctive	Preterite	Imperfect	Future	Conditional
yo	voy	vaya	fui	iba	iré	iría
tú	vas	vayas	fuiste	ibas	irás	irías
él, ella, usted	va	vaya	fue	iba	irá	irías
nosotros, nosotras	vamos	vayamos	fuimos	íbamos	iremos	iríamos
vosotros, vosotras	vais	vayáis	fuisteis	ibais	iréis	iríais
ellos, ellas, ustedes	van	vayan	fueron	iban	irán	irían

F. *Oír* (to hear)

Infinitive: **oír**   Gerund: **oyendo**   Past Participle: **oído**
Imperative: **oye (tú); no oigas (tú); oiga (usted)**

	Present Indicative	Present Subjunctive	Preterite	Imperfect	Future	Conditional
yo	oigo	oiga	oí	oía	oiré	oiría
tú	oyes	oigas	oíste	oías	oirás	oirías
él, ella, usted	oye	oiga	oyó	oía	oirá	oiría
nosotros, nosotras	oímos	oigamos	oímos	oíamos	oiremos	oiríamos
vosotros, vosotras	oís	oigáis	oísteis	oíais	oiréis	oiríais
ellos, ellas, ustedes	oyen	oigan	oyeron	oían	oirán	oirían

G. *Poder* (can; to be able to)

Infinitive: **poder**   Gerund: **pudiendo**   Past Participle: **podido**

	Present Indicative	Present Subjunctive	Preterite	Imperfect	Future	Conditional
yo	puedo	pueda	pude	podía	podré	podría
tú	puedes	puedas	pudiste	podías	podrás	podrías
él, ella, usted	puede	pueda	pudo	podía	podrá	podría
nosotros, nosotras	podemos	podamos	pudimos	podíamos	podremos	podríamos
vosotros, vosotras	podéis	podáis	pudisteis	podíais	podréis	podríais
ellos, ellas, ustedes	pueden	puedan	pudieron	podían	podrán	podrían

H. *Querer* (to want)

Infinitive: **querer**   Gerund: **queriendo**   Past Participle: **querido**

	Present Indicative	Present Subjunctive	Preterite	Imperfect	Future	Conditional
yo	quiero	quiera	quise	quería	querré	querría
tú	quieres	quieras	quisiste	quería	querrás	querrías
él, ella, usted	quiere	quiera	quiso	querías	querrá	querría
nosotros, nosotras	queremos	queramos	quisimos	quería	querremos	querríamos
vosotros, vosotras	queréis	queráis	quisisteis	queríamos	querréis	querríais
ellos, ellas, ustedes	quieren	quieran	quisieron	querían	querrán	querrían

LEARN TO SPEAK SPANISH

I. *Ser* (to be)

Infinitive: **ser**   Gerund: **siendo**   Past Participle: **sido**
Imperative: **sé (tú); no seas (tú); sea (usted)**

	Present Indicative	Present Subjunctive	Preterite	Imperfect	Future	Conditional
yo	soy	sea	fui	era	seré	sería
tú	eres	seas	fuiste	eras	serás	serías
él, ella, usted	es	sea	fue	era	será	sería
nosotros, nosotras	somos	seamos	fuimos	éramos	seremos	seríamos
vosotros, vosotras	sois	seáis	fuisteis	erais	seréis	seríais
ellos, ellas, ustedes	son	sean	fueron	eran	serán	serían

J. *Saber* (to know)

Infinitive: saber   Gerund: sabiendo   Past Participle: sabido
Imperative: sabe (tú); no sepas (tú); sepa (usted)

	Present Indicative	Present Subjunctive	Preterite	Imperfect	Future	Conditional
yo	sé	sepa	supe	sabía	sabré	sabría
tú	sabes	sepas	supiste	sabías	sabrás	sabrías
él, ella, usted	sabe	sepa	supo	sabía	sabrá	sabría
nosotros, nosotras	sabemos	sepamos	supimos	sabíamos	sabremos	sabríamos
vosotros, vosotras	sabéis	sepáis	supisteis	sabíais	sabréis	sabríais
ellos, ellas, ustedes	saben	sepan	supieron	sabían	sabrán	sabrían

K. *Tener* (to have)

Infinitive: **tener**   Gerund: **teniendo**   Past Participle: **tenido**

Imperative: **ten (tú); no tengas(tú); tenga (usted)**

	Present Indicative	Present Subjunctive	Preterite	Imperfect	Future	Conditional
yo	tengo	tenga	tuve	tenía	tendré	tendría
tú	tienes	tengas	tuviste	tenías	tendrás	tendrías
él, ella, usted	tiene	tenga	tuvo	tenía	tendrá	tendría
nosotros, nosotras	tenemos	tengamos	tuvimos	teníamos	tendremos	tendríamos
vosotros, vosotras	tenéis	tengáis	tuvisteis	teníais	tendréis	tendríais
ellos, ellas, ustedes	tienen	tengan	tuvieron	tenían	tendrán	tendrían

L. *Venir* (to come)

Infinitive: **venir**   Gerund: **viniendo**   Past Participle: **venido**

Imperative: **ven (tú); no vengas (tú); vengas (usted)**

	Present Indicative	Present Subjunctive	Preterite	Imperfect	Future	Conditional
yo	vengo	venga	vine	venía	vendré	vendría
tú	vienes	vengas	viniste	venías	vendrás	vendrías
él, ella, usted	viene	venga	vino	venía	vendrá	vendría
nosotros, nosotras	venimos	vengamos	vinimos	veníamos	vendremos	vendríamos
vosotros, vosotras	venís	vengáis	vinisteis	veníais	vendréis	vendríais
ellos, ellas, ustedes	vienen	vengas	vinieron	venían	vendrán	vendrían

M . *Ver* (to see)

Infinitive: **ver** Gerund: **viendo** Past Participle: **visto**
Imperative: **ve (tú); no veas (tú); vea (usted)**

	Present Indicative	Present Subjunctive	Preterite	Imperfect	Future	Conditional
yo	veo	vea	vi	veía	veré	vería
tú	ves	veas	viste	veías	verás	verías
él, ella, usted	ve	vea	vio	veía	verá	vería
nosotros, nosotras	vemos	veamos	vimos	veíamos	veremos	veríamos
vosotros, vosotras	veis	veáis	visteis	veíais	veréis	veríais
ellos, ellas, ustedes	ven	vean	vieron	veían	verán	verían

V. STEM-CHANGING VERBS

Stem-changing verbs follow the conjugation patterns but have a slight spelling change in their stems. Common verbs in this category include *pensar*, *pedir* and *volver*.

A. *Pensar* (to think): e>ie

The *e* in the stem of these verbs becomes *ie* in the present indicative and subjunctive except in the first and second person plurals (*nosotros* and *vosotros*). Notice that all of these verbs end in either *–ar* or *–er*.

	Present Indicative	Present Subjunctive
yo	pienso	piense
tú	piensas	pienses
él, ella, usted	piensa	piense
nosotros, nosotras	pensamos	pensemos
vosotros, vosotras	pensáis	penséis
ellos, ellas, ustedes	piensan	piensen

Other verbs that follow this pattern: *cerrar, comenzar, despertar, empezar, entender, perder, preferir**.

*-*Ir* verbs that belong to this category, like *preferir*, will also carry a stem-change in the preterite forms of the third person singular and plural, changing their *–e* into *–i*: *él prefirió*; *ellos prefirieron*.

B. *Pedir* (to ask for): e>i

These verbs, which all end in *–ir*, change the *e* in their stem to *ie* in the present indicative and subjunctive as well as in the preterite. Notice that the changes occur in all of the subjunctive forms, only in the singular forms and third person plural in the present indicative tense and in the third person forms in the preterite.

	Present Indicative	Present Subjunctive	Preterite
yo	pido	pida	pedí
tú	pides	pidas	pediste
él, ella, usted	pide	pida	pidió
nosotros, nosotras	pedimos	pidamos	pedimos
vosotros, vosotras	pedís	pidáis	pedisteis
ellos, ellas, ustedes	piden	pidan	pidieron

Other verbs conjugated like *pedir: repetir, seguir, servir, vestirse.*

C. *Volver* (to return): o or u>ue

These verbs change the *o* or *u* in their stems to *ue* in the present indicative and subjunctive in all the persons except in the first and second plural forms (*nosotros, vosotros*).

	Present Indicative	Present Subjunctive
yo	vuelvo	vuelva
tú	vuelves	vuelvas
él, ella, usted	vuelve	vuelva
nosotros, nosotras	volvemos	volvamos
vosotros, vosotras	volvéis	volváis
ellos, ellas, ustedes	vuelven	vuelvan

Other verbs conjugated like *volver: almorzar, acordarse, contar, costar, dormir*, encontrar, jugar**.*

*Dormir also has a stem-change in the preterite forms of the third person singular and plural: *él durmió, ellos durmieron.*

**Jugar changes its *u* to *ue*.

VI. SPELLING CHANGES

Some verbs, like those ending in *–car*, *–gar*, and *–zar* as well as the verb *conocer*, experience spelling changes to form the present subjunctive tense.

	buscar (to look for): *c>qu*	*conocer* (to know): *c>zc*	*empezar* (to begin): *z>c*	*pagar* (to pay): *g>gu*
yo	busque	conozca	empiece	pague
tú	busques	conozcas	empieces	pagues
él, ella, usted	busque	conozca	empiece	pague
nosotros, nosotras	busquemos	conozcamos	empecemos	paguemos
vosotros, vosotras	busquéis	conozcáis	empecéis	paguéis
ellos, ellas, ustedes	busquen	conozcan	empiecen	paguen

All of these verbs, except *conocer*, present the same spelling change in the first person singular of the preterite form: *yo busqué, yo empecé, yo pagué.* The verb *conocer* changes its stem in the first person singular of the present indicative tense: *yo conozco.*

APPENDIX B: GRAMMAR GLOSSARY

TERM	DEFINITION	EXAMPLES
adjective	A word used to describe a person or a thing. Adjectives agree in gender and number with the nouns they modify.	**la casa** *azul* the *blue* house **el perro grande** the big dog
adverb	A word that qualifies a verb, an adjective, another adverb, or a phrase.	**Ella corrió** *rápidamente.* She ran *quickly.* **Él es** *muy* **simpático.** He's *very* nice.
adverb of place	An adverb which describes spatial relationships.	*a la derecha* *right* *arriba* *above*
adverb of time	An adverb which describes relationships of time.	*una vez* *once* *ahora* *now* *ya* *already*
adverbial phrase	A phrase that acts as an adverb. **(See "adverb" and "phrase.")**	**Miró el libre con** *un vivo interés.* He looked at the book *with keen interest.*
affirmation	A positive statement. The opposite of negation. **(See also "negation.")**	*Se compraron una nueva casa.* *They bought a new house.*
article	A word that characterizes an item (person, thing, or idea) as definite or indefinite. **(See also "definite article" and "indefinite article.")**	*la* **casa** *the* house *un* **automóvil** *a* car
article word	A word that characterizes an item with reference to the speaker (definite, indefinite, closer, further, interrogative, etc).	*el, un, este* *the, a, this*
attributive adjective	An adjective that describes a noun and is not separated from the noun by the verb.	**La casa** *azul* **está en llamas.** The *blue* house is on fire.
cardinal number	A number used to count. **(See "ordinal number.")**	*cinco, quince* *five, fifteen*

clause	A distinct part of a sentence which includes a subject and a predicate (with a verb). **(See also "independent clause" and "subordinate clause.")**	*Fui al mercado* **(clause)** *porque necesitaba leche* **(clause).** *I went to the market* (clause), *because I needed milk* (clause).
command	The form of the verb used to give a command or an order. **(See also "imperative.")**	*Salga!* *Go* outside! *Sal!*
comparative	A degree of comparison of adjectives and adverbs. The comparative implies a comparison of only two items (people, things, or ideas) or two groups of items. **(See also "superlative.")**	**Este libro es *más interesante que* la película.** This book is *more interesting than* the movie.
conditional	The conditional is used to express the result of a hypothetical condition or supposition.	**Si viera un fantasma, me *desmayaría*.** If I saw a ghost I *would* faint.
conjugation	The system of verb forms that expresses person, number, tense, and mood.	*yo veo* . . . .*I see* *tú verás* . . . . .*you will see* *él/ella vio* . . . .*he/she saw* *usted veía* . . . .*you were seeing* *nosotros veremos* . . . .*we will see* *vosotros veíais* . . . .*you were seeing* *ellos/ellas* *habían visto* . .*they had seen* *ustedes vieron* .*you saw*
conjunction	A word that links together words, clauses, and even sentences. **(See also "coordinating conjunction" and "subordinating conjunction.")**	*y* . . . .*and* *o* . . . .*or* *pero* . . . .*but*

contraction	A form produced by the shortening of a syllable, word, or word group by leaving out a sound or letter.	**Nosotros venimos *del* (de + el) hospital.** We are coming from the hospital. **Él va *al* (a + el) cine.** He is going to the movies.
coordinating conjunction	A conjunction that links independent clauses or sentences. **(See also "subordinating conjunction.")**	**Yo cociné *y* mi hermana fregó los platos.** I cooked *and* my sister washed the dishes.
definite article	A word used to indicate a specific item (person, thing, or idea), an idea that is modified in some fashion or an item that stands for all objects of its kind.	*la* **casa** *the* house
demonstrative adjective	An adjective or article word that indicates, shows, or points out the noun it modifies.	*Esta* **casa.** *This* house.
demonstrative pronoun	A pronoun that replaces a noun or noun phrase that is indicated, shown, or pointed out.	*Eso* **no me gusta.** I don't like *that*. **Es *éste* el que él te dio?** Is *this the one* he gave you?
dependent clause	**(See "subordinate clause.")**	
dependent infinitive phrase	A dependent phrase which uses the infinitive of a verb and "to" or "in order to" to express the purpose of an action.	**Tuve que tomar un taxi *para ir al aeropuerto*.** I had to take a taxi in *order to reach the airport*.
direct object	The person or thing directly acted upon by the verb. In Spanish, when the direct object is a person, it must be preceded by the preposition **a**.	**José limpió *la cocina*.** José cleaned *the kitchen*. **Llamé a *Margarita* anoche.** I called *Margarita* last night.
ending	One or more letters or syllables added to a word base.	**escuch*ado*** . . . . .listen*ed* **cant*ando*** . . . . .sing*ing*
exclamatory expression	A sudden utterance used to express emotion or catch attention.	*Oye*! *Hey*!

future	A verb tense which refers to events that take place after the present.	*Iré* **dentro de un mes.** I *will go* in a month.
gender	A grammatical classing of nouns into masculine and feminine.	*el libro (m.)* ...the book /*la casa (f.)* ....the house
helping verb	A verb which is used to conjugate another verb.	**Ya** *habíamos* **visto esa película.** We *had* already seen this film.
imperative mood	**(See "command.")**	
imperfect	A verb tense primarily used to express progressive actions, repetitive actions, or to describe events in the past.	*Comía* **carne todas las noches.** I *used to* eat meat every night.
indefinite article	A word that is used to indicate an item (person, thing, or idea) that is not specified in any particular way, or is not known to the listener.	**Tiene** *un* **automóvil.** He has *a* car. *Una* **niña se cayó de su bicicleta.** *A* little girl fell from her bike.
independent clause	A clause that expresses a self-contained complete idea.	*Comí un sandwich.* *I ate a sandwich.*
indicative mood	A mood which states a fact or makes a declaration with reference to the writer or speaker.	*Hablo español.* *I speak Spanish.*
indirect object	The person or thing indirectly affected by the verb.	**Le di la flor** *a mi mamá.* I gave the flower *to my mother*.
infinitive	The basic form of a verb as given in a dictionary.	*hablar* .... *to speak* *comer* .... *to eat*
infinitive noun	A noun which is formed from the infinitive form of a verb. An infinitive noun means "the act of" whatever the verb signifies.	*Fumar* **es peligroso para la salud.** *Smoking* is hazardous to your health.
interrogative	A word used to ask a question. In Spanish, interrogative words have a written accent.	*quién* .... *who* *qué* .... *what*

interrogative adjective	An adjective used to ask a question. In Spanish, interrogative words have a written accent.	***cuál*** . . . . *which*
intonation	The rhythm and voice pitch of spoken speech.	
irregular verb	A verb with a non-standard conjugation pattern. (See also "regular verb.")	**ser** . . . .*to be* **yo *soy*** . . . .*I am* **tú *eres*** . . . .*you are* **él/ella *es*** . . . .*he/she is* **usted *es*** . . . .*you are* **nosotros *somos*** . .*we are* **vosotros *sois*** .*you are* **ellos/ellas *son*** . . .*they are* **ustedes *son*** . . . . . .*you are*
linking element	A sound or word used to start a sentence, allowing the speaker to focus attention on what is about to be said, and giving the speaker extra time to formulate his or her thoughts.	***Bueno***. . . . .*Well. . .* ***Entonces***. . . . . . .*So. . .* ***Este***. . . . .*Hmm. . .*
main clause	The part of the sentence which expresses the main idea, and which can stand alone. **(See also "subordinate clause")**	***Comí un sandwich* porque tenía hambre.** *I ate a sandwich* because I was hungry.
mood	A form of the verb which distinguishes whether the action or state expressed by the verb is perceived as fact or not. **(See also "subjunctive," "indicative," and "command.")**	***Como verduras.*** — **indicative mood.** *I eat vegetables.* **Quiero *que tú comas verduras.*** — **subjunctive mood.** I want you to eat vegetables
negation	A denial; the opposite of affirmation. **(See also "affirmation.")**	*No* **compraron una nueva casa.** They *didn't* buy a new house.
noun	A word used to name a person, place, thing, or idea.	la ***mujer*** the *woman* esta ***casa*** this *house* un ***automóvil*** a *car* la ***belleza*** beauty

number	A term used to distinguish between singular, which refers to one of something, and plural, which refers to more than one of something.	
numerical adjective	A word which gives estimated numbers rather than specific ones.	*muchos* . . . . *many* *algunos* . . . .*a few*
ordinal number	A number used to place people or things in a serial order. (**See also "cardinal number."**)	*quinto* . . . .*fifth* *noveno* . . . .*ninth*
participle	An adjective derived from a verb.	**la ventana cerrada** the *closed* window **una vela encendida** a *lit* candle
particle	A minor part of speech such as an article or a demonstrative adjective.	*un* . . . .*a* *este* . . . .*this*
passive voice	A form of the verb used when the subject of the sentence is acted upon, instead of doing the action.	**El reporte *fue leído* por el Señor Ramírez.** The report *was read* by Mr. Ramírez.
past	A verb tense which refers to events that take place before the present, with reference to the writer or speaker.	***Vi* esa película ayer.** I *saw* that movie yesterday. ***Estaba nevando.*** It *was snowing.* **Ya *había puesto* la mesa cuando *llamaste.*** I *had already set* the table when you *called.*
past participle	A form of the verb used either as an adjective or to form compound tenses.	**Lo ha *dicho.*** He has *said* it. **La puerta está *cerrada.*** The door is *closed.*
past perfect	A verb tense which denotes a time before a reference point in the past, with reference to the writer or speaker.	**Ya *había puesto* la mesa cuando *llamaste.*** I *had already* set the table when you *called.*

person	Reference to the person speaking, the person being spoken to, or the person being spoken about.	**first person—*yo, nosotros, nosotras*** first person -- *I, we* **second person—*tú, usted, vosotros, vosotras, ustedes*** second person -- *you, sing. & pl., formal & informal* **third person—*él, ella, ellos, ellas*** third person -- *he, she, it/they*
personal sphere adverb	(See "adverb of place.")	
phrase	A cluster of words without a conjugated verb.	**Fui *a la tienda.*** I went *to the store.*
plural	Refers to more than one of something.	
polite conditional	The use of the conditional to make a request.	***¿Podría hablar más despacio?*** *Could* you speak more slowly?
possessive adjective	An adjective which indicates to whom or what something or someone pertains or belongs.	***mi* libro** . . . .*my* book ***su* perro** . . . .*his* dog
possessive pronouns	A pronoun which indicates to whom or what something or someone pertains or belongs.	**Tu casa es roja. *La mía* es blanca.** Your house is red. *Mine* is white.
predicate	The part of the sentence which tells you about the subject. It generally consists of a verb, objects, and anything which modifies the verb.	**Pedro *lavó su ropa ayer.*** Pedro *washed his clothes yesterday.*
prefix	A particle added to the beginning of a word to change its meaning.	***predecir*** to predict
preposition	A word or words which express location, time, or direction.	*en* . . . .*in* *para* . . . .*for* *a través de* . . . . .*through*

present	A verb tense used for activities which occur at the present time, in the near future, or which are habitual, with reference to the speaker or writer.	**Como verduras todos los días.** I *eat* vegetables every day.
preterit	(See "simple past.")	
pronoun	A word which replaces a noun or a noun phrase in naming a person or a thing.	**Pedro está enfermo.** *Pedro* is sick. **Él está enfermo.** *He* is sick.
question	An interrogative sentence or clause which is normally used to gain information. In Spanish, questions are surrounded by interrogative signs (¿?).	**¿Dónde está el baño?** *Where is the bathroom?*
question word	(See "interrogative.")	
reflexive pronoun	An object pronoun which refers to the subject.	**Él se afeita.** He shaves *himself.* **Ella se levanta.** She wakes up.
reflexive verb	A verb used with a reflexive pronoun.	**Me levanto a las siete de la mañana.** I wake up at 7:00 AM.
regular verb	A verb which follows standard rules for verb conjugation. **(See also "irregular verb.")**	**hablar** . . . ."talk" **yo** . . . .*hablo* . . . .I *talk* **tú** . . . .*hablas* . . .you *talk* **él/ella** . . .*habla* . . . .he/she/it *talks* **usted** . . . .*habla* . . . .you *talk* **nosotros** . .*hablamos* we *talk* **vosotros** . .*habláis* . .you *talk* **ellos/ellas** .*hablan* . . .they *talk* **ustedes** . . .*hablan* . . .you *talk*
relative pronoun	A pronoun which relates or links a subordinate clause to a main clause.	**Conocí a la mujer *que* escribió esta novela.** I met the woman *who* wrote this novel.

sentence structure	(see "word order")	
simple past	A verb tense used to express completed actions in the past. It is most commonly used in writing. The "simple past" is the same as the "preterite."	***Fui*** **al cine anoche.** I *went* to the movies yesterday.
singular	Refers to one of something.	
social register	The language that is appropriate to a particular subject, person, and occasion.	
stem	The basic form of a verb or a noun after all prefixes, suffixes, and endings are removed.	***camin-*** **(ar)** . . . .*walk* ***com-*** **(er)** . . . . . .*eat*
subject	A word or group of words within a sentence that perform the action denoted by the verb.	***El perro*** **mordió al cartero.** *The dog* bit the mailman.
subject pronoun	A pronoun which functions as the subject of the sentence. Because most verb endings in Spanish tell who is doing the action, it is not necessary to use the subject pronoun in most cases.	***(Ella)*** **se compró un nuevo automóvil.** *She* bought a new car.
subjunctive mood	A mood which expresses uncertainty, possibility, a hypothesis, a condition, a hope, a wish, etc.	**Quiero que** ***comas*** **verduras.** I *want* you to eat vegetables.
subordinate clause	A clause that depends on a main clause to be complete.	**Comí un sandwich** ***porque tenía hambre.*** I ate a sandwich *because I was hungry.*
subordinating conjunction	A word used to link clauses, one of which depends for its full meaning on the main clause. (**See also "coordinating conjunction."**)	***que*** . . . .*that* ***si*** . . . .*if* ***a menos que*** . . . .*unless* ***porque*** . . . .*because*

suffix	A particle added to the end of a word to change its meaning.	*rápidamente* *quickly*
superlative	The highest degree of some quality. The superlative implies a comparison of more than two items or groups of items.	**Él piensa que Nueva York es *la mejor ciudad* del mundo.** He thinks New York is *the best city* in the world.
tense	A form of a verb which expresses different times as perceived by the speaker. **(See also "present," "imperfect," "perfect," and "future".)**	
verb	A word that typically expresses action, state, or a relation between two things, and that may be conjugated for person, tense, and mood. The main element of the predicate.	***Quiero* mucho a mis hijos.** I *love* my children. **Mi hermano *trabaja* con computadoras.** My brother *works* with computers.
word order	The sequence of words in a sentence.	

Indices
DIALOGUES INDEX

GRAMMAR INDEX